MARCO ⊕ POLO

SPANISH

● Spanish = official language

> Words are wonderful – they let us connect with each other, experience new worlds, and live life to the full.

In this book, we've collected together all the key terms and phrases you'll need so that you'll never be lost for words during your adventures in a foreign culture and with a foreign language.

With our cheat sheet, you'll always be ready to deal with any linguistic surprises that come your way.

And if you're still stuck for words, our 'point & show' pictures are an easy way to keep on communicating.

Have a wonderful trip!

How much is it?
¿Cuánto cuesta?
[kwanto kwessta]

> PRONUNCIATION MADE EASY

Don't be shy, just get stuck in: our simple phonetic pronunciation guides will help you pronounce all the words, terms and phrases in this book easily and correctly.

> 'POINT & SHOW' PICTURES

A picture is worth a thousand words. Whether you're out shopping, in a restaurant, at a hotel or need help with your car, our 'point & show' pictures will help you on your way.

> INSTANT INFORMATION

FROM A TO Z
All the key themes in alphabetical order: from Doctor's visits to telephone conversations.

DICTIONARY
An A to Z of the most important words. How handy!

KEY EXPRESSIONS AT A GLANCE .... INSIDE COVER
CHEAT SHEET | NUMBERS, WEIGHTS & MEASURES | THE TIME | DIRECTIONS

COLOURS, PATTERNS & MATERIALS 4

PRONUNCIATION 5

PLANNING YOUR TRIP... 6
BOOKING BY EMAIL 6 ACCOMMODATION ENQUIRIES 8

BASIC CONVERSATION... 10
TIME 16 THE WEATHER 19

OUT & ABOUT 20
HOW DO I GET TO...? 20 AT THE BORDER 22 TRAVELLING BY CAR/MOTORBIKE/
BICYCLE 23 TRAVELLING BY PLANE 30 TRAVELLING BY TRAIN 31
TRAVELLING BY BOAT 33 PUBLIC TRANSPORT 34 LIFT SHARING 35

FOOD & DRINK... 36
GOING FOR A MEAL 36 THE MENU 46 THE DRINKS MENU 52

SHOPPING 54

WHERE TO STAY... 68
GENERAL INFORMATION 68 AT A HOTEL 69 IN A HOLIDAY HOME 74
AT A CAMPSITE 76 AT A YOUTH HOSTEL 77

CONTENTS

> MENUS

Order with ease and tuck in with pleasure – foreign language menus will never be an indecipherable mystery again.

> A PACKED SCHEDULE

Do you want culture, adventure, theatre, diving trips, or language and cooking classes? We've got phrases to make your trip even more exciting.

> LOCAL KNOWLEDGE

Insider Tips To help you pass for an insider, not just a tourist.

DOS AND DON'TS!
Help you to avoid faux pas.

WARNING! SLANG
Understand the locals better!

A PACKED SCHEDULE 78
GENERAL INFORMATION 78 SIGHTSEEING/MUSEUMS 79 TRIPS & TOURS 81
AFTER DARK 82 AT THE BEACH & SPORTS 84 COURSES 89

WARNING! SLANG 90
DAY TO DAY 92 FOOD 95 GOING OUT 95 MEN & WOMEN 97
RANTING, BITCHING, SWEARING 98 UNMENTIONABLES 100 MONEY 100
WORK 101 THE WEATHER 102

CREDITS 103

FROM A TO Z 104
BANK/BUREAU DE CHANGE 104 COLOURS 106 AT THE DOCTOR'S 107
INTERNET CAFÉS 113 LOST & FOUND 113 MAIL 114 ON THE PHONE 114
TAKING PHOTOS 116 POLICE 117 TOILETS & BATHROOMS 118
TRAVELLING WITH KIDS 119

DICTIONARY 120

DOS & DON'TS! 136

KEY EXPRESSIONS AT A GLANCE .... INSIDE COVER
PARDON? | KEY QUESTIONS

The colours, patterns and materials below are handy for shopping trips.
You'll find more help for (almost!) every situation throughout this book.

PRONUNCIATION

To make life easier, we've included a simple pronunciation guide after all the Spanish words and phrases in this book. Just pronounce most of the sounds exactly as you would if you were reading them in English.

There are a few sounds in Spanish that English speakers don't say very often (if at all). But don't worry – just bear the following notes in mind as you go along and you'll be sounding like a local in no time:

the vowels 'e' and 'o' – when you say '**e**', make it sound like the flat 'e' in the English words '**met**' and '**bed**'. The '**o**' should be pronounced as in the English word '**bone**'.

r – 'r's in Spanish are rolled/trilled. Single 'r's in the middle of words are only trilled lightly. When you come across double 'r's and single 'r's at the start of words, however, you can really go to town!

kh – we've used this letter combination to represent the throaty sound Spanish speakers make when they pronounce '**j**'s and some '**g**'s. It's pronounced in the back of the throat like the 'ch' sound in the Scottish word "Lo**ch**" (i.e. Loch Ness).

ai – represents the sound of the English word '**eye**' – e.g. 'el aire' [el ai-reh] ("air").

ow – in this book, pronounce this sound as it appears in the English sentence "**how now brown cow**" (and not "below").

y – when you see this letter in the pronunciation guide, always pronounce it like the '**y**' in "**yes**", and not like the 'y' in "my".

hyphens – hyphens have been used to make the pronunciation guide easier to read. All the sounds connected by hyphens should be joined together when you say them out loud.

stress – there are a few simple rules for placing the stress on Spanish words. Words ending in '**n**', '**s**' or any of the vowels are stressed on the second-to-last syllable. Words ending in all other consonants are stressed on the final syllable. Any exceptions to these rules are shown with an accent over the letter that needs to be stressed: e.g. caf**é**, despu**é**s, etc.

MASCULINE OR FEMININE?

Spanish words come in two genders: masculine and feminine. But don't worry: it's usually very easy to tell them apart. That's because words ending in 'o' (plural = 'os') tend to be masculine, while words ending in 'a' (plural = 'as') are usually feminine. The genders of any exceptions to these rules, and of any words ending in different letters, will be shown in this book. This will be done either by including an m or an f after the word, or by writing the appropriate Spanish words for 'a' (un m and una f) and 'the' (singular: el m and la f; plural: los m and las f) in front.

There are various ways of saying 'you' in Spanish. Use *usted* [oossted] (singular) and *ustedes* [oosstedess] (plural) when talking to people you don't know well or in formal situations. When you get to know people better, use *tú* [too] (singular) and *vosotros/vosotras* (plural).

Note: The phonetics in this book represent the 'standard' version of Spanish. When listening to other varieties of the language, you will often hear the 'th' sound replaced with an 'ss'.

ABBREVIATIONS

adj	adjective (adjetivo)	f	feminine (femenina, femenino)
adv	adverb (adverbio)	pl	plural (plural)
sth	something (algo)	alg	alguien (someone)
m	masculine (masculina, masculino)	s.o.	someone (alguien)

> SEA VIEWS AND EXTRA BEDS

Whether you want a dreamy seaside hotel or an extra bed in your room: arrange it all by email, by fax or over the phone and you can go on holiday relaxed in the knowledge that everything's sorted out.

BOOKING BY EMAIL

HOTEL | HOTEL [otel]

Dear Sir/Madam,
I would like to reserve a (single/double/twin) bedroom from the 28th to the 30th of June.
I would be grateful if you could tell me whether or not you have a room free for these nights, and what the price would be (including breakfast).
Best wishes,

PLANNING YOUR TRIP

Apreciados señores:

Quisiera reservar una habitación (sencilla/doble/con dos camas) para las noches del 28 y 29 de junio. Hagan el favor de comunicarme si tienen habitaciones libres para esas fechas y el precio por noche (más desayuno). Atentamente,

RENTAL CARS | COCHE DE ALQUILER [kocheh deh alkeeler]

Dear Sir/Madam,
I would like to rent a small car/midrange car/(7-seater) minivan from Barajas (Madrid) airport from the 20th to the 25th of July. I would like to return the car to Barcelona, as my return

flight leaves from there. Could you please send me your prices and let me know which documents I will require?
Best wishes,

Apreciados señores:
Quisiera alquilar un coche pequeño/de tamaño medio/de (siete plazas) del 20 al 25 de julio en el aeropuerto de Barajas (Madrid) y devolverlo en Barcelona, ya que el vuelo de regreso lo hago desde allí. Les estaría agradecido si me informaran de las tarifas y de los documentos que es necesario presentar.
Atentamente,

ACCOMMODATION ENQUIRIES

I'm looking for a nice hotel/bed and breakfast (with good food) in the old town.

Estoy buscando un hotel bonito/un alojamiento con desayuno en el casco antiguo/viejo (que tenga una buena cocina). [esstoy boosskando oon otel boneeto/oon alokha-mee-ento kon dessa-yoono en el kassko anteegwo/bee-ekho (keh tenga oona bwena kotheena)]

Is it central/quiet/near the beach?

¿Está cerca del centro/en un sitio tranquilo/cerca de la playa? [essta therka del thentro/en oon seet-yo trankeelo/therka deh la pla-ya]

How much does it cost per week?

¿Cuánto cuesta a la semana? [kwanto kwessta a la semana]

Can you find this accommodation on the Internet?

¿Tiene el alojamiento una dirección de internet? [tyeneh el alokha-mee-ento oona deerek-thyon deh eenternet]

a hotel — un hotel [oon otel]
a guest house — una pensión [oona penssyon]
a room — una habitación [oona abeetath-yon]
a holiday apartment — un apartamento [oon apartamento]

HOTEL/GUEST HOUSE/ROOMS
HOTEL/PENSIÓN/HABITACIONES [otel/penssyon/abeetathee-yoness]

▶ Where to Stay: page 68

I'd like to stay in a hotel, but nothing too expensive – something mid-priced.

Busco un hotel, pero que no sea muy caro, de tipo medio. [boossko oon otel, pero keh no saya mwee karo, deh teepo med-yo]

I'm looking for a hotel with...	Busco un hotel con … [boossko oon otel kon]
a swimming pool.	piscina. [peess-theena]
a golf course.	campo de golf. [kampo deh golf]
tennis courts.	pistas de tenis. [peesstass deh teneess]
Can you give me a quiet room/ a room with a view/ a room with a balcony?	¿Podría darnos una habitación tranquila/una habitación con vistas/una habitación con balcón? [podree-a darnoss oona abeetath-yon trankeela/oona abeetath-yon kon beesstass/oona abeetath-yon kon balkon]
Is it possible to put an extra bed in the room?	¿Se puede poner otra cama en la habitación? [seh pwedeh poner otra kama en la abeetath-yon]

HOLIDAY HOMES/HOLIDAY APARTMENTS
CASAS/APARTAMENTOS [kassass/apartamentoss]

 Where to Stay: page 74

I'm looking for an apartment or a bungalow.	Busco un apartamento o un bungaló. [boossko oon apartamento o oon boongalo]
Is there...?	¿Tiene …? [tyeneh]
a kitchen	una cocina [oona kotheena]
a dishwasher	lavavajillas [labava-khee-yass]
a refrigerator	un frigorífico/una nevera [oon freegoreefeeko/oona nebera]
a washing machine	lavadora [labadora]
a TV	televisor m [telebeessor]
Wi-Fi	(conexión f) wifi [(konekssyon) wai-fai]
Is electricity included in the price?	¿Va la luz incluida en el precio? [ba la looth eenkloo-eeda en el preth-yo]
Are bed linen and towels provided?	¿Hay ropa de cama y toallas? [ai ropa deh kama ee to-a-yass]
How much deposit do you require and when do I have to pay it?	¿Qué paga y señal hay que hacer y cuándo? [keh paga ee senyal ai keh ather ee kwando]
Where and when should I pick up the keys?	¿Dónde y cuándo puedo recoger la llave? [dondeh ee kwando pwedo rekokher la yabeh]

CAMPING | CAMPING [kampeeng]

I'm looking for a nice campsite (on the waterfront).	Busco un camping bonito (en la orilla). [boossko oon kampeeng boneeto (en la oree-ya)]
Is there anything you can recommend?	¿Cuál me recomendaría? [kwal meh rekomendaree-a]

> EXPERIENCE MORE

Don't be shy! Whether it's small talk in a café, chatting away
on a shopping trip or flirting in a club – just get stuck in!
It's easier than you think and a great way to spice up your trip!

■■SAYING HELLO | SALUDO [saloodo] ■■■■■■■■■■■■■■■■

Good morning!	¡Buenos días! [bwenoss dee-ass]
Good afternoon!	¡Buenos días!/¡Buenas tardes! [bwenoss dee-ass/bwenass tardess]
Good evening!	¡Buenas tardes!/¡Buenas noches!
	[bwenass tardess/bwenass nochess]
Hello!/Hi!	¡Hola!/¿Qué tal? [ola/keh tal]
How are you?	¿Qué tal está usted? [keh tal essta oossted]
Good, thanks.	Bien, gracias. [byen, grath-yass]
And you?	¿Y usted/tú? [ee oossted/too]

BASIC CONVERSATION

■ MY NAME IS... | ME LLAMO ... [meh yamo] ■

What's your name?	¿Cómo se llama usted? [komo seh yama oossted]/
	¿Cómo te llamas? [komo teh yamass]
Nice to meet you!	¡Mucho gusto en conocerle!
	[moocho goossto en konotherleh]
May I introduce you?	Le/Te presento …
This is...	[leh/teh pressento]
Ms X./Mr X.	a la señora X./al señor X. [a la senyora X/al senyor X]
my partner.	mi pareja. [mee parekha]

■GOODBYE/BYE! | ¡HASTA LA VISTA!/¡ADIÓS! [assta la beessta/ad-yoss]

Bye!/See you later!	¡Adiós!/¡Hasta luego! [ad-yoss/assta lwego]
See you tomorrow!/soon!	¡Hasta mañana!/¡pronto! [assta manyana/pronto]
Good night!	¡Buenas noches! [bwenass nochess]
It was nice to meet you.	Me alegro mucho de haberle/haberte conocido.
	[meh alegro moocho deh aberleh/aberteh konotheedo]

■PLEASE | POR FAVOR [por fabor]

Could you do me a favour?	¿Puedo pedirle un favor? [pwedo pedeerleh oon fabor]
Can you help me, please?	¿Puede usted ayudarme, por favor?
	[pwedeh oossted a-yoodarmeh, por fabor]
May I?	¿Permite? [permeeteh]
Don't mention it.	De nada. [deh nada]
You're welcome.	No hay de qué. [no ai deh keh]
With pleasure!	¡Con (mucho) gusto! [kon (moocho) goossto]

■THANK YOU! | ¡GRACIAS! [grath-yass]

Thank you very much!	¡Muchas gracias! [moochass grath-yass]
Yes, thank you!	¡Gracias, con mucho gusto! [grath-yass, kon moocho goossto]
No, thank you!	No, muchas gracias. [no, moochass grath-yass]
Thank you. The same to you!	Gracias, igualmente. [grath-yass, eegwalmenteh]
That's very kind of you,	Gracias, es muy amable de su/tu parte.
thank you.	[grath-yass, ess mwee amableh deh soo/too parteh]

■I'M SORRY! | ¡PERDÓN! [perdon]

I'm sorry (I'm late)!	¡Lo siento mucho! (¡Siento mucho llegar tarde!)
	[lo syento moocho (syento moocho yegar tardeh)]
What a pity!	¡Peccato! [pek'kato]

■ALL THE BEST! | ¡QUE LE/TE VAYA BIEN! [keh leh/teh ba-ya byen]

Congratulations!	¡Mi más cordial felicitación!/¡Enhorabuena!
	[mee mass kord-yal feleetheetath-yon/enorabwena]
Happy birthday!	¡Muchas felicidades en el día de su/tu cumpleaños!
	[moochass feleetheedadess en el dee-a deh soo/too koomplay-anyoss]
Good luck!	¡Mucho éxito!/¡Mucha suerte! [moocho eksseeto/moocha swerteh]

BASIC CONVERSATION

■COMPLIMENTS | CUMPLIDOS [koompleedoss]

How nice/lovely!	¡Qué bien! [keh byen]
That's wonderful/great!	¡Esto es fantástico! [essto ess fantassteeko]
You speak very good English.	Habla muy bien el inglés. [abla mwee byen el eengless]
You look very nice!	¡Está usted muy guapo/guapa! [essta oossted mwee gwapo/gwapa]
I think you're very nice.	Lo/La encuentro muy simpático/simpática/amable.
	[lo/la enkwentro mwee seempateeko/seempateeka/amableh]

beautiful	bonito [boneeto]
excellent	excelente [ekss-thelenteh]
friendly	amable [amableh]
impressive	impresionante [eempressyonanteh]
nice	agradable [agradableh]
pretty	(person) guapo [gwapo]; (object) bonito [boneeto]
tasty	bueno [bweno], rico [reeko]
wonderful	fantástico [fantassteeko]

LOCAL KNOWLEDGE

¡Hola!

Insider Tips

▶ Greetings
The Spanish are very relaxed when it comes to saying 'hello'. Of course you'll hear the more standard *Buenos días* [bwenoss dee-ass] until about 2pm, *Buenas tardes* [bwenass tardess] until around 9pm and *Buenas noches* later on at night, but you'll come across the more casual alternatives – ¡*Hola!* [ola] "Hello!", and ¿*Qué tal?/¿Qué hay?* [keh tal/key ay] "How's it going?"

▶ See You Later?
When saying goodbye, Spanish people often use casual phrases that – if taken literally – sound as if they're making arrangements for a future date. But don't get out your diary straight away: when someone says *Hasta luego* [assta loo-ego] or *Nos vemos* [noss bemoss] ("till later" and "we'll see each other", respectively), it doesn't necessarily mean they have any plans to see you in the future. Equally, when someone says *Nos llamamos* [noss yamamos] ("we'll speak on the phone"), they might have no intention of ever dropping you a line.

▶ Forms of Address
To address someone politely or in a formal context, use the polite form of you (*usted* [oossted]) along with *señor* or *señora: Buenos días, señor/señora López, ¿cómo se encuentra usted?* [bwenoss dee-ass, senyor/senyora lopeth, como she enkwentra oossted]. This is also the right way of going about asking an older person for directions, etc.: *Perdone señora/señor, ¿dónde se encuentra el hotel ...?* [peroneh senyora/senyor, doneh se enkwentra el otel]

PERSONAL INFORMATION SOBRE SU PERSONA [sobreh soo perssona]

What do you do for a living?	¿Qué profesión tiene usted/tienes?
	[keh professyon tyeneh oossted/tyeness]
I'm a...	Soy … [soy]
I work in...	Trabajo en … [trabakho en]
I'm still at school.	Todavía voy al colegio. [todabee-a boy al kolekh-yo]
I'm a student.	Soy estudiante. [soy esstood-yanteh]
How old are you?	¿Qué edad tiene usted/tienes? [keh edad tyeneh oossted/tyeness]
I'm (twenty-four).	Tengo (veinticuatro) años. [tengo (bayntee-kwatro) anyoss]

ORIGIN AND STAY LUGAR DE ORIGEN Y DOMICILIO [loogar deh oreekhen ee domeetheelyo]

Where do you come from?	¿De dónde es usted/eres? [deh dondeh ess oossted/eress]
I'm from (London).	Soy de (Londres). [soy deh (londress)]
I'm from England.	Vengo d'Inglaterra. [bengo deenglatera]
Have you been here long?	¿Lleva usted/Llevas ya mucho tiempo aquí?
	[yeba oossted/yebass ya moocho tyempo akee]
I've been here since...	Estoy aquí desde … [esstoy akee dezdeh]
How long are you staying?	¿Cuánto tiempo se queda/te quedas?
	[kwanto tyempo seh keda/teh kedass]
Do you like it?	¿Qué le parece? [keh leh paretheh]
What's your e-mail address?	¿Me da/das tu dirección electrónica/de e-mail?
	[meh da/dass too deerek-thyon elektroneeka/deh eemail]

HOBBIES HOBBIES [khob-eess]

What do you do in your spare time?	¿Qué hace usted/haces en tu tiempo libre?
	[keh atheh oossted/athess en too tyempo leebreh]
I'm interested in art/culture/architecture/fashion.	Me interesa … el arte/cultura/arquitectura/moda.
	[meh eenteressa … el arteh/kooltoora/arkeetektoora/moda]
Are you on Facebook?	¿Tiene/tienes cuenta en facebook?
	[tyeneh/tyeness kwenta en fayss-book]
cards/board games	los juegos de naipes/de mesa
	[loss khwegoss deh naipess/deh messa]
cinema/movies	el cine/las películas [el theeneh/lass peleekoolass]
computer games	los juegos de ordenador
	[loss khwegoss deh ordenador]
cooking	cocinar [kotheenar]
learning languages	aprender idiomas [aprender eed-yomass]
listening to music	escuchar música [esskoochar moosseeka]
making music	hacer música [ather moosseeka]
meeting friends	salir con los amigos
	[saleer kon loss ameegoss]

BASIC CONVERSATION

painting	pintar [peentar]
reading	leer [lay-er]
taking photos	fotografiar [fotograf-yar]
travelling	viajar [bee-akhar]

SPORT DEPORTE [deporteh]

 A Packed Schedule: page 85

What sports do you do?	¿Qué deporte practica usted? [keh deporteh prakteeka oossted]
I play...	Juego a … [khwego a]
football/tennis/volleyball/	fútbol [footbol]/tenis [teneess]/voleibol [bolaybol]/
handball/table tennis.	balonmano [balom-mano]/tenis de mesa. [teneess deh messa]
I go to the gym/	Voy a menudo al gimnasio (Am: fitness)/a practicar
to yoga regularly.	yoga. [boy a menoodo al kheemnassyo (feet-ness)/a prakteekar yoga]
I go jogging/swimming/	Corro./Nado./Voy en bicicleta.
cycling.	[koro/nado/boy en beetheekleta]

MAKING A DATE | CITA/LIGUE [theeta/leekheh]

Have you got any plans for tomorrow evening?	¿Tiene usted/Tienes algún plan para mañana por la noche? [tyeneh oossted/tyeness algoon plan para manyana por la nocheh]
Shall we meet up this evening?	¿Quedamos esta tarde/noche? [kedamoss essta tardeh/nocheh]
When shall we meet?	¿A qué hora nos encontramos? [a keh ora noss enkontramoss]
Can I take you home?	¿Puedo acompañarla/acompañarle/acompañarte a casa? [pwedo akompanyarla/akompanyarleh/akompanyarteh a kassa]
Have you got a boyfriend/ a girlfriend?	¿Tienes novio/novia? [tyeness nob-yo/nob-ya]
Are you married?	¿Está usted casado/casada? [essta oossted kassado/kassada]
I've been looking forward to seeing you all day.	Le/Te he esperado con impaciencia todo el día. [leh/teh eh essperado kon eempath-yenth-ya todo el dee-a]
You've got beautiful eyes!	Tienes unos ojos bellísimos. [tyeness oonoss okhoss bay-eess-eemoss]
I love you!	¡Te quiero! [teh kyero]
I've fallen in love with you.	Me he enamorado de ti. [meh eh enamorado deh tee]
I've fallen in love with you, too.	Yo también de ti. [yo tam-byen deh tee]
I would like to sleep with you.	Quiero pasar la noche contigo. [kyero passar la nocheh konteego]
But only if we use a condom!	¡Pero solo con condón! [pero solo kon kondon]
Do you have condoms?	¿Tienes condones? [tyeness kondoness]
Where can I buy some?	¿Dónde se compran? [dondeh seh kompran]
I don't want to.	No quiero. [no kyero]
Please leave now!	¡Por favor, vete ahora! [por fabor, beteh a-ora]
Stop immediately!	¡Basta ya! [bassta ya]

| Go away!/Get lost! | ¡Lárgate! [largateh] |
| Please leave me alone! | ¡Por favor, déjeme en paz! [por fabor, dekhemeh en path] |

TIME

■ TIME | LA HORA [la ora]

WHAT TIME IS IT? ¿QUÉ HORA ES? [keh ora ess]

 Time: Inside front cover

WHAT TIME?/WHEN? ¿A QUÉ HORA?/¿CUÁNDO? [a keh ora/kwando]

At (one) o'clock.	A la (una). [a la (oona)]
In (one hour's) time.	Dentro de (una) hora. [dentro deh (oona) ora]
Between (three) and (four).	Entre las (tres) y las (cuatro). [entreh lass (tress) ee lass (kwatro)]

HOW LONG? ¿CUÁNTO TIEMPO? [kwanto tyempo]

Two hours.	Dos horas. [doss orass]
From (ten) to (eleven).	Desde las (diez) hasta las (once). [dezdeh lass (dyeth) assta lass (ontheh)]
Until (five) o'clock.	Hasta las (cinco). [assta lass (theenko)]

SINCE WHEN? ¿DESDE CUÁNDO? [dezdeh kwando]

| Since (eight am). | Desde las (ocho de la mañana).
[dezdeh lass (ocho deh la manyana)] |
| For half an hour. | Desde hace media hora. [dezdeh atheh med-ya ora] |

■ OTHER EXPRESSIONS OF TIME
■ OTRAS INDICACIONES DE TIEMPO [otrass eendeekath-yoness deh tyempo]

in the morning	por la mañana [por la manyana]
during the morning	por la mañana [por la manyana]
at lunchtime	a mediodía [a med-yo-dee-a]
in the afternoon	por la tarde [por la tardeh]
in the evening	por la tarde [por la tardeh]
at night	por la noche [por la nocheh]

the day before yesterday	anteayer [antay-a-yer]
yesterday	ayer [a-yer]
ten minutes ago	hace diez minutos [atheh dyeth meenootoss]

BASIC CONVERSATION

today	hoy [oy]
now	ahora [a-ora]
tomorrow	mañana [manyana]
the day after tomorrow	pasado mañana [passado manyana]
this week	esta semana [essta semana]
at the weekend	el fin de semana [el feen deh semana]
on Sunday	el domingo [el domeengo]
in a fortnight's time	dentro de quince días [dentro deh keentheh dee-ass]
next year	el año que viene [el anyo keh bee-eneh]
sometimes	a veces [a bethess], algunas veces [algoonass bethess]
every half hour	cada media hora [kada med-ya ora]
every hour	cada hora [kada ora]
every day	a diario [a dyar-yo], todos los días [todoss loss dee-ass]
every other day	cada dos días [kada doss dee-ass]
within a week	en una semana [en oona semana]
soon	pronto [pronto]

▮THE DATE | FECHA [fecha]

What's the date today?	¿Qué día es hoy? [keh dee-a ess oy]/
	¿A cuánto estamos? [a kwanto esstamoss]
Today's the first of May.	Hoy es el primero/el uno de mayo.
	[oy ess el preemero/el oono deh ma-yo]

▮DAYS OF THE WEEK | LOS DÍAS DE LA SEMANA [loss dee-ass deh la semana]

Monday	el lunes [el looness]
Tuesday	el martes [el martess]
Wednesday	el miércoles [el mee-erkoless]
Thursday	el jueves [el khweh-bess]
Friday	el viernes [el bee-erness]
Saturday	sábado [sabado]
Sunday	domingo [domeengo]

▮MONTHS OF THE YEAR | LOS MESES [loss messess]

January	enero [enero]
February	febrero [febrero]
March	marzo [martho]
April	abril [abreel]

May	mayo [ma-yo]
June	junio [khoon-yo]
July	julio [khool-yo]
August	agosto [agossto]
September	septiembre [sept-yembreh]
October	octubre [oktoobreh]
November	noviembre [nob-yembreh]
December	diciembre [deeth-yembreh]

■SEASONS | LAS ESTACIONES DEL AÑO [lass esstath-yoness del anyo]

spring	primavera [preemabera]
summer	verano [berano]
autumn/fall	otoño [otonyo]
winter	invierno [eem-bee-erno]

■HOLIDAYS | LOS DÍAS DE FIESTA/FESTIVOS [loss dee-ass deh fyessta/fessteeboss]

New Year's Day	año nuevo [anyo nwebo]
Epiphany	el Día del Reyes [el dee-a del ray-ess]
Saint Joseph's Day (19th of March)	San José [san khosseh]
Maundy Thursday	el Jueves Santo [el khwebess santo]
Good Friday	el Viernes Santo [el bee-erness santo]
Easter	Pascua (de Resurrección) [passkwa (deh ressoorek-thyon)]
Easter Monday	el Lunes de Pascua [el looness deh passkwa]
Labor Day (1st of May)	el Día del Trabajo [el dee-a del trabakho]
Ascension	La Ascensión [la ass-thenssyon]
Pentecost	Pentecostés [pentekosstess]
The Feast of Corpus Christi	el Corpus (Christi) [el korpooss (chreesstee)]
St John's Eve (23rd of June)	San Juan [san khwan]
Columbus Day (12th of Oct; national holiday)	el Día de la Hispanidad [el dee-a deh la eesspaneedad]
Assumption Day	La Asunción [la assoonth-yon]
All Saints' Day (1st of Nov)	Todos los Santos [todoss loss santoss]
All Souls' Day (2nd of Nov)	el Día de los Difuntos [el dee-a deh loss deefoontoss]
Constitution Day (6th of Dec)	el Día de la Constitución [el dee-a deh la konssteetooth-yon]
Immaculate Conception (8th of Dec)	la Inmaculada (Am: el Día de la Virgen) [la eem-makoolada (el dee-a deh la beerkhen)]
Christmas Eve	Nochebuena [nochebwena]
Christmas	la Navidad [la nabeedad]
New Year's Eve	Nochevieja [noche-bee-ekha]

THE WEATHER

What's the weather going to be like today?	¿Qué tiempo tendremos hoy? [keh tyempo tendremoss oy]
It's going to stay fine/remain poor.	Seguirá el buen/mal tiempo. [segeera el bwen/mal tyempo]
It's going to get warmer/colder.	Va a hacer más calor/más frío. [ba a ather mass kalor/mass free-o]
It's going to rain/snow.	Va a llover/nevar. [ba a yober/nebar]
It's cold/hot/close.	Estamos a frío/calor/bochorno. [esstamoss a free-o/kalor/bochorno]
What's the temperature today?	¿Qué temperatura hace hoy? [keh temperatoora atheh oy]
It's (20) degrees.	Hace (veinte) grados. [atheh (baynteh) gradoss]

air	el aire [el ai-reh]
changeable	inestable [eenesstableh]
climate	el clima [el kleema]
close/muggy/oppressive	bochornoso [bochornosso]
cloud	la nube [la noobeh]
cloudy	nublado [nooblado]
cold	frío [free-o]
drought	sequía [sekee-a]
flood	la inundación [la eenoondath-yon]
fog	niebla [nyebla]
frost	helada [elada]
heat	el calor [el kalor]
high tide	marea alta [maraya alta]
(very) hot	(muy) cálido [(mwee) kaleedo], (muy) caluroso [(mwee) kaloorosso]
lightning	rayo [ra-yo]
low tide	marea baja [maraya bakha]
rain	lluvia [yoob-ya]
rainy	lluvioso [yoob-yosso]
snow	la nieve [la nyebeh]
sun	el sol [el sol]
sunny	soleado [solay-ado]
temperature	temperatura [temperatoora]
thunder	trueno [troo-eno]
thunderstorm	tormenta [tormenta]
warm	caliente [kal-yenteh], cálido [kaleedo]
wet	húmedo [oomedo]
wind	viento [bee-ento]

> WHICH WAY TO THE...?

If you're lost, confused, or simply don't know where to go:
ask someone! This chapter will help you get back on track.

HOW DO I GET TO...?

Excuse me, where's..., please?	Perdón, ¿dónde está …? [perdon, dondeh essta]
Excuse me, how do you get to...?	¿Podría decirme cómo se va a …? [podree-a detheermeh komo seh ba a]
What's the quickest way to...?	¿Cuál es el camino más corto para ir a …? [kwal ess el kameeno mass korto para eer a]
How far is it?	¿A qué distancia está? [a keh deesstanth-ya essta]
Go straight on.	Todo seguido (Am: derecho). [todo segeedo (derecho)]

OUT AND ABOUT

Turn left/right.	Tuerza (Am: Doble) a la izquierda/derecha. [too-ertha [dobleh] a la eeth-kyerda/derecha]
The first/second street on the left/right.	La primera/segunda calle a la izquierda/a la derecha. [la preemera/segoonda ka-yeh a la eeth-kyerda/a la derecha]
Cross... the bridge./ the square./the street.	Atraviese … el puente./la plaza./la calle. [atrab-yesseh … el pwenteh/la platha/la ka-yeh]
Then ask again.	Luego pregunte usted otra vez. [lwego pregoonteh oossted otra beth]
You can take...	Puede usted tomar … [pwedeh oossted tomar]
the bus.	el autobús. [el owtobooss]
the tram.	el tranvía. [el trambee-a]
the tube (the underground).	el metro (Am: el subterráneo). [el metro [el soobteranayo]]

AT THE BORDER

CUSTOMS/PASSPORT CONTROL DUANAS/CONTROL DE PASAPORTES [adwanass/kontrol deh passaportess]

Your passport, please!
¡Su pasaporte, por favor! [soo passaporteh, por fabor]

Your passport has expired.
Su pasaporte está caducado. [soo passaporteh essta kadookado]

Have you got a visa?
¿Tiene usted un visado (Am: una visa)?
[tyeneh oossted oon beessado (oona beessa)]

Can I get a visa here?
¿Puedo conseguir un visado (Am: una visa) aquí mismo? [pwedo konsseger oon beessado (oona beessa) akee meezmo]

Have you got anything to declare?
¿Tiene usted algo que declarar?
[tyeneh oossted algo keh deklarar]

Pull over to the right, please.
Aparque aquí a la derecha, por favor.
[aparkeh akee a la derecha, por fabor]

Open the...
¿Quiere abrir ..., por favor? [kyereh abreer ..., por fabor]

boot (trunk)/this case, ...please.
el portaequipajes (Am: el baúl) [el porta-ekeepakhess (el ba-ool])/esta maleta (Am: valija) [essta maleta (baleekha)]

Do I have to pay duty on this?
¿Hay que pagar derechos de aduana por esto?
[ai keh pagar derechoss deh adwana por essto]

Christian name, first name	el nombre [el nombreh]
customs	aduana [adwana]
date of birth	fecha de nacimiento [fecha deh nathee-mee-ento]
driving licence	permiso/el carné de conducir [permeesso/el karneh deh kondootheer]
duty-free	exento de derechos de aduana [ekssento deh derechoss deh adwana]
enter the country	entrar en el país [entrar en el pa-eess]
export	la exportación [la ekssportath-yon]
ID card	el carné/documento de identidad (Am: cédula personal) [el karneh/dokoomento deh eedenteedad (sedoola perssonal)]
import	la importación [la eemportath-yon]
leave the country	salir de un país [saleer deh oon pa-eess]
liable to customs duty	sujeto a derechos de aduana [sookheto a derechoss deh adwana]
maiden name	el nombre de soltera [el nombreh deh soltera]
marital status	estado civil [esstado theebeel]
married	casado [kassado]
nationality	la nacionalidad [la nath-yonaleedad]
passport	el pasaporte [el passaporteh]
place of birth	el lugar de nacimiento [el loogar deh natheemee-ento]
place of residence	domicilio [domeetheel-yo]
single	soltero [soltero], soltera [soltera]
surname	el apellido [el apayeedo]
valid	válido [baleedo]
visa	visado (Am: visa) [beessado (beessa)]

TRAVELLING BY CAR/MOTORBIKE/BICYCLE

■HOW DO I GET TO...? | ¿CÓMO SE VA A ...? [komo seh ba a]

How far is it?	¿A qué distancia está? [a keh deesstanth-ya essta]
Excuse me, is this the road to...?	Perdón, ¿es esta la carretera de ...? [perdon, ess essta la karetera deh]
How do I get to the motorway to...?	¿Cómo se va a la autopista de ...? [komo seh ba a la owtopeessta deh]
Straight on until you get to... Then turn left/right.	Todo seguido (Am: derecho) hasta ... Luego tuerza (Am: doble) a la izquierda/derecha. [todo segeedo (derecho) assta ... lwego too-ertha (dobleh) a la eeth-kyerda/derecha]

■FILL UP THE TANK, PLEASE
LLENO, POR FAVOR [yeno, por fabor]

Where's the nearest petrol/ gas station, please?	¿Dónde está la estación de servicio/la gasolinera más cercana, por favor? [dondeh essta la esstath-yon deh serbeeth-yo/ la gassoleenera mass therkana, por fabor]
95 octane/98 octane/diesel; charging point for electric vehicles	gasolina normal/súper/diesel; puntos de recarga para coches (Am: autos) eléctricos/electrocoche/electroauto [gassoleena normal/sooper/dyessel/poontoss deh rekarga para kochess (owtoss) elektreekoss/elektrokocheh/elektro-owto]
Please check the oil/ the tyre/tire pressure.	¿Quiere comprobar el nivel del aceite?/ la presión de las ruedas? [kyereh komprobar el neebel del athay-teh/ la pressyon deh lass rwedass]
Could you also check the radiator water, please?	Controle también el agua del radiator, por favor. [kontroleh tam-byen el agwa del rad-yator, por fabor]
Where is the toilet, please?	¿Dónde está el baño/servicio? [dondeh essta el banyo/serbeeth-yo]

■PARKING | APARCAMIENTO [aparka-mee-ento]

Excuse me, is there a car park/ parking lot near here?	Perdón, ¿hay algún sitio para aparcar por aquí cerca? [perdon, ai algoon seet-yo para aparkar por akee therka]
Can I park my car here?	¿Puedo dejar el coche aquí? [pwedo dekhar el kocheh akee]

■ BREAKDOWN | AVERÍA [aberee-a]

Could you help me jump-start my car?	¿Podría utilizar los cables de arranque con su coche (Am: auto)? [podree-a ooteelee-thar loss kabless deh arankeh kon soo kocheh [owto]]
Would you send a breakdown truck, please?	¿Pueden ustedes enviarme un grúa? [pweden oosstedess emb-yarmeh oon groo-a]
Could you give me some petrol/gas, please?	¿Podría usted darme un poco de gasolina, por favor? [podree-a oossted darmeh oon poko deh gassoleena, por fabor]
Could you help me change the tyre/tire, please?	¿Podría usted ayudarme a cambiar la rueda? [podree-a oossted a-yoodarmeh a kamb-yar la rweda]
Could you tow me to the nearest garage?	¿Puede usted remolcarme hasta el taller más próximo? [pwedeh oossted remolkarmeh assta el ta-yer mass proksseemo]

■ GARAGE | EL TALLER [el ta-yer]

The car won't start.	Mi coche no arranca. [mee kocheh no aranka]
Could you have a look?	¿Puede usted mirar, por favor? [pwedeh oossted meerar, por fabor]
The battery is flat.	La pila está agotada. [la peela essta agotada]
There's something wrong with the engine.	El motor no funciona bien. [el motor no foonth-yona byen]
The brakes don't work.	Los frenos no funcionan bien. [loss frenoss no foonth-yonan byen]
...is/are faulty.	... está/están estropeado/s. [essta/esstan esstropay-ado/-adoss]
I'm losing oil.	El coche pierde aceite. [el kocheh pyerdeh athay-teh]
Change the sparkplugs, please.	Cambie las bujías, por favor. [kamb-yeh lass bookhee-ass, por fabor]
How much will it cost?	¿Cuánto costará? [kwanto kosstara]

■ ACCIDENTS | UN ACCIDENTE [oon aktheedenteh]

Please call...	Llame enseguida ... [yameh enssegeeda]
an ambulance.	una ambulancia. [oona amboolanth-ya]
the police.	a la policía. [a la poleethee-a]
the fire brigade.	a los bomberos. [a loss bombeross]
Are you injured?	¿Está (usted) herido/herida? [essta (oossted) ereedo/ereeda]
Have you got a first-aid kit?	¿Tiene usted botiquín de urgencias? [tyeneh oossted boteekeen deh oor-khenth-yass]
It was my fault.	Ha sido por mi culpa. [a seedo por mee koolpa]
It was your fault.	Ha sido por su culpa. [a seedo por soo koolpa]
Shall we call the police, or can we settle things ourselves?	¿Llamamos a la policía o lo arreglamos entre nosotros? [yamamoss a la poleethee-a o lo areglamoss entreh nossotross]

Please give me your name and address.	¿Puede usted darme su nombre y dirección? [pwedeh oossted darmeh soo nombreh ee deerek-thyon]
Please give me the name and address of your insurance company.	¿Puede usted darme el nombre y dirección de su compañía de seguros? [pwedeh oossted darmeh el nombreh ee deerek-thyon deh soo kompanyee-a deh segooross]
Thank you very much for your help.	Muchas gracias por su ayuda. [moochass grath-yass por soo a-yooda]

accelerator	el pedal del gas [el pedal del gass]
alcohol level	por mil [por meel]
automatic (transmission)	caja de cambios automática [kakha deh kamb-yoss owtomateeka]
backfire	encendido defectuoso [enthendeedo defekt-wosso]
battery	pila [peela], batería [bateree-a]
bell	el timbre [el teembreh]
bend (in a road, etc.)	curva [koorba]
bicycle rack	el portabicicletas [el portabeetheekletass]
bicycle, bike	bicicleta [beetheekleta]
body, bodywork	carrocería [karotheree-a]
brake pad	ferodo [ferodo]
breakdown	avería [aberee-a]
breakdown service	servicio de ayuda al automovilista [serbeeth-yo deh a-yooda al owtomobeeleessta]
breakdown/tow truck	grúa [groo-a]
broken	roto [roto]
cable	el cable [el kableh]
car park (parking lot)	aparcamiento (Am: parqueadero) [aparka-mee-ento (parkaya-dero)]
car wash	lavado del coche [labado del kocheh]
carburettor	el carburador [el karboorador]

LOCAL KNOWLEDGE

Insider Tip

Operation Vacation

On the 1st, 15th, and 30th of August, the whole of Spain is either going on holiday or coming back home. That means you'd better think twice about travelling anywhere on these dates! Such is the upheaval that the Spanish have coined military-sounding names for their summertime to-ing and fro-ing: *Operación Salida* [operath-yon saleeda] ("Operation Departure") and *Operación Retorno* [operath-yon retorno] ("Operation Return"). Easter and the first weekend in May are also traditionally characterised by completely jam-packed roads and an increase in road traffic accidents.

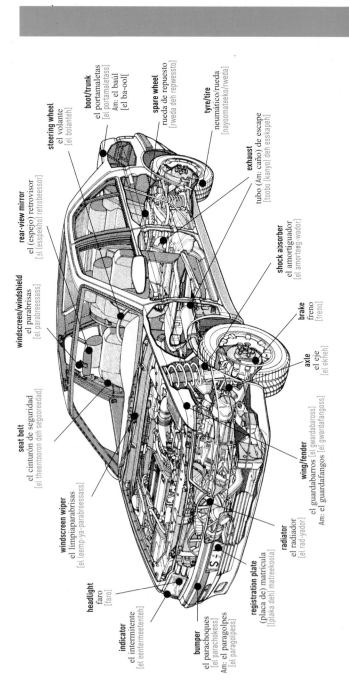

boot/trunk
el portamaletas
[el portamaletass]
Am: el baúl
[el ba-ool[

spare wheel
rueda de repuesto
[rweda deh repwessto]

tyre/tire
neumático/rueda
[nayoomateeko/rweda]

steering wheel
el volante
[el bolanteh]

rear-view mirror
el (espejo) retrovisor
[al (esspekho) retrobeessor]

exhaust
tubo (Am: caño) de escape
[toobo (kanyo) deh esskapeh]

shock absorber
el amortiguador
[el amorteeg-wador]

windscreen/windshield
el parabrisas
[el parabreessass]

brake
freno
[freno]

axle
el eje
[el ekheh]

seat belt
el cinturón de seguridad
[el theentooron deh segoreedad]

wing/fender
el guardabarros [el gwardabaross]
Am: el guardafangos [el gwardafangoss]

windscreen wiper
el limpiaparabrisas
[el leemp-ya-parabreessass]

radiator
el radiador
[el rad-yador]

registration plate
(placa de) matrícula
[(plaka deh) matreekoola]

headlight
faro
[faro]

indicator
el intermitente
[el eentermeetenteh]

bumper
el parachoques
[el parachokess]
Am: el paragolpes
[el paragolpess]

clutch	el embrague [el embrageh]
coolant	(el) agua del radiador [(el) agwa del rad-yador]
country road	carretera [karetera]
crash helmet	casco [kassko]
crossroads, junction	el cruce de calles f [el krootheh deh ka-yess]
dimmed beam headlights	la luz de cruce [la looth deh krootheh]
diversion/detour	la desviación [la dessbee-ath-yon]
driving licence	permiso/el carné de conducir [permeesso/el karneh deh kondootheer]
dynamo/alternator	la dínamo [la deenamo]
emergency telephone	el poste de socorro [el possteh deh sokoro]
fan belt	correa trapezoidal (Am: correa en V) [koraya trapethoy-dal (koraya en beh)]
fault n	avería [aberee-a], defecto [defekto]
fine	multa [moolta]
flat tyre (tire)/puncture	pinchazo [peenchatho]
footbrake	freno de pie [freno deh pyeh]
fuel pump	bomba de gasolina [bomba deh gassoleena]
fuel station for electric cars	punto de recarga de electricidad [poonto deh rekarga deh elektreetheedad]
full/high beam lights	la luz de carretera [la looth deh karetera]
fully comprehensive insurance	seguro a todo riesgo [segooro a todo ree-ezgo]
fuse	el fusible [el foosseebleh]
garage	el taller [el ta-yer]
gasket	junta [khoonta]
gear	marcha [marcha], la velocidad [la belotheedad]
gearbox	caja de cambio [kakha deh kamb-yo]
gearstick	palanca de cambio [palanka deh kamb-yo]
green card (insurance)	carta verde (del seguro) [karta berdeh (del segooro)]
handbrake	freno de mano [freno deh mano]
hazard warning light	el sistema de alarma intermitente [el seesstema deh alarma eentermeetenteh]
heating	la calefacción [la kalefak-thyon]
hitch-hiker	autoestopista m/f [owto-esstopeessta]
horn	bocina [botheena], el claxon [el klaksson]
horsepower, hp	caballos de vapor, CV [kaba-yoss deh bapor, theh-beh]
ignition	encendido (Am: la ignición) [enthendeedo (la eegneess-yon)]
ignition key	la llave de encendido [la yabeh deh enthen-deedo]
ignition switch	cerradura de contacto [theradoora deh kontakto]
jack	gato [gato], el alzacoches [altha-kochess]
jump lead	el cable de ayuda para el arranque [el kableh deh a-yooda para el arankeh]
lane	pista [peessta]
lorry, truck	el camión [el kam-yon]
motor, engine	el motor [el motor]

motorbike	la moto(cicleta) [la moto(theekleta)]
motorway service station (rest stop)	el albergue de carretera [el albergeh deh karetera]
motorway/highway	autopista [owto-peessta]
mudguard	el guardabarros (Am: el guardafangos) [el gwardabaross (el gwardafangoss)]
multi-storey car park/ parking lot	el garaje de varios pisos [el garakheh deh bar-yoss peessoss]
natural gas (LPG) station	la estación de gas natural [la esstath-yon deh gass natooral]
octane number	número de octanos [noomero deh oktanoss], el octanaje [el oktana-kheh]
oil, oil change	el aceite [el athay-teh], cambio de aceite [kamb-yo deh athay-teh]
papers (documents)	los documentos [loss dokoomentoss]
petrol/gas	gasolina [gassoleena]
petrol/gas can	el bidón (Am: el tanque) de gasolina [el beedon (el tankeh) deh gassoleena]
petrol/gas station	gasolinera [gassoleenera], la estación de servicio [la esstath-yon deh serbeeth-yo]
pump	bomba de aire [bomba deh ai-reh]
(puncture) repair kit	los parches y el pegamento [loss parchess ee el pegamento]
radar speed check	el control de radar [el kontrol deh radar]
raincoat	chubasquero [choobasskero]
rim	llanta [yanta]
road map	el mapa de carreteras [el mapa deh kareterass]

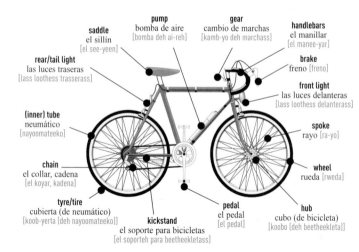

pump bomba de aire [bomba deh ai-reh]

gear cambio de marchas [kamb-yo deh marchass]

handlebars el manillar [el manee-yar]

saddle el sillín [el see-yeen]

rear/tail light las luces traseras [lass loothess trasserass]

brake freno [freno]

front light las luces delanteras [lass loothess delanterass]

(inner) tube neumático [nayoomateeko]

spoke rayo [ra-yo]

chain el collar, cadena [el koyar, kadena]

wheel rueda [rweda]

tyre/tire cubierta (de neumático) [koob-yerta (deh nayoomateeko)]

kickstand el soporte para bicicletas [el soporteh para beetheekletass]

pedal el pedal [el pedal]

hub cubo (de bicicleta) [koobo (deh beetheekleta)]

road works	(las) obras [(lass) obrass]
scooter	el escúter [el esskooter], el scooter [el skooter]
screw	tornillo [tornee-yo]
short-circuit	cortocircuito [korto-theer-kweeto]
sidelights	la luz de población/estacionamiento [la looth deh poblath-yon/esstath-yona-mee-ento]
spanner, wrench	la llave de tuercas [la yabeh deh too-erkass]
spark plug	bujía [bookhee-a]
speedometer	el cuentakilómetros [el kwentakeelo-metross], velocímetro [belothee-metro]
starter	el motor de arranque [el motor deh arankeh]
street, road	la calle [la ka-yeh]
sunroof	techo corredizo [techo koredeetho]
toll (charge)	el peaje [el pay-akheh]
tools	las herramientas [lass era-mee-entass]
tow (away)	remolcar [remolkar]
towrope	el cable de remolque [el kableh deh remolkeh]
traffic jam	atasco [atassko], embotellamiento [embotaya-mee-ento]
traffic lights	semáforo [semaforo], disco [deessko]
valve	válvula [balboola]
warning triangle	la señal de situación de peligro [la senyal deh seetoo-ath-yon deh peleegro], triángulo de peligro [tree-angoolo deh peleegro]

CAR/MOTORBIKE/BICYCLE HIRE
ALQUILER DE AUTOMÓVILES/MOTOS/BICICLETAS

I'd like to hire... for (2) days/for (a week). a car/a camper van/ a scooter/a motorbike/ a bicycle	Quisiera alquilar por (dos) días/(una) semana … [keessyera alkeelar por (doss) dee-ass/(oona) semana] el coche (Am: auto)/autocaravana/vespa/ motocicleta/bicicleta [el kocheh (owto)/owtokarabana/ besspa/mototheekleta/beetheekleta]
I'd like an automatic/ air-conditioning/ a navigation system.	Por favor con cambio de marchas automático/ aire acondicionado/GPS (Am: navegador). [por fabor kon kamb-yo deh marchass owtomateeko/ai-reh akondeeth-yonado/kheh-peh-esseh (nabegador)]
How much does it cost per day/week?	¿Qué tarifa se paga por un día/por una semana? [keh tareefa seh paga por oon dee-a/por oona semana]
What do you charge per km?	¿Cuánto se paga por cada kilómetro de recorrido? [kwanto seh paga por kada keelometro deh rekoreedo]
Does the vehicle have comprehensive insurance?	¿Está el vehículo asegurado a todo riesgo? [essta el bay-eekoolo assegoorado a todo ree-ezgo]
Is it possible to return the car in/at...?	¿Es posible entregar el vehículo en …? [ess posseebleh entregar el bay-eekoolo en]

TRAVELLING BY PLANE

DEPARTURE | EL DESPEGUE [el desspekheh]

Where's the counter for (name of airline)?	¿Dónde está la facturación de …? [dondeh essta la faktoorath-yon deh]
When's the next flight to...?	¿A qué hora sale el próximo avión para …? [a keh ora saleh el proksseemo ab-yon para]
I'd like to book a single flight to...	Quisiera reservar un vuelo de ida a … [keessyera resserbar oon bwelo deh eeda a]
Are there still seats available?	¿Hay todavía plazas libres? [ai todabee-a plathass leebress]
I'd like to change the flight.	Quisiera cambiar el vuelo. [keessyera kamb-yar el bwelo]
When do I have to be at the airport?	¿A qué hora tengo que estar en el aeropuerto? [a keh ora tengo keh esstar en el ai-ro-pwerto]
Can you check in for the flight the night before/ over the phone/ online?	¿Se ofrece un servicio de facturación la noche anterior/por teléfono/por internet para este vuelo? [seh ofretheh oon serbeeth-yo deh faktoorath-yon la nocheh anter-yor/por telefono/por eenternet para essteh bwelo]
Can I take this this on as hand luggage/baggage?	¿Puedo llevar esto como equipaje de mano? [pwedo yebar essto komo ekeepakheh deh mano]
Is the plane to... late?	¿Tiene retraso el avión a …? [tyeneh retrasso el ab-yon a]

ARRIVAL | LLEGADA [yegada]

My luggage/baggage is missing.	Mi equipaje se ha perdido. [mee ekeepakheh seh a perdeedo]
My suitcase has been damaged.	Mi maleta (Am: valija) está rota. [mee maleta (baleekha) essta rota]

airline	compañía aérea [kompanyee-a a-er-aya]
airport bus	el autobús del aeropuerto [el owtobooss del ai-ro-pwerto]
baggage/luggage claim	entrega de equipaje [entrega deh ekeepakheh]
(boarding) gate	puerta [pwerta]
boarding card	tarjeta de embarque [tarkheta deh embarkeh]
booking	reserva [resserba]
cancel	anular [anoolar]
change (a flight)	cambiar (el vuelo) [kamb-yar (el bwelo)]
check in v	facturar [faktoorar]
connection	el empalme [el empalmeh]
counter	ventanilla [bentanee-ya]
delay	retraso [retrasso]
departure	el despegue [el desspegeh]
direct flight	vuelo directo [bwelo deerekto]

duty-free shop	venta libre de impuestos [benta leebreh deh eempwesstoss]
e-ticket	el billete electrónico [el bee-yeteh elektroneeko]
emergency chute/slide	el tobogán de emergencia [el tobogan deh emer-khenth-ya]
emergency exit	salida de emergencia [saleeda deh emer-khenth-ya]
emergency landing	el aterrizaje forzoso [el ateree-thakheh forthosso]
fasten your seatbelt	abrocharse el cinturón de seguridad [abrocharsseh el theentooron deh segooreedad]
flight	vuelo [bwelo]
(hand) luggage/baggage	el equipaje (de mano) [el ekeepakheh (deh mano)]
landing	el aterrizaje [el atereethakheh]
life jacket	chaleco salvavidas [chaleko salbabeedass]
luggage/baggage claim	la facturación de equipajes [la faktoorath-yon deh ekeepakhess]
on board	a bordo [a bordo]
online booking	reserva/compra en internet [resserba/kompra en eenternet]
passenger	pasajero [passakhero]
pilot	el/la piloto [el/la peeloto]
plane	el avión [el ab-yon]
route	ruta (de vuelo) [roota (deh bwelo)]
scheduled time of departure	salida regular [saleeda regoolar]
seatbelt	el cinturón de seguridad [el theentooron deh segooreedad]
security control	el control de seguridad [el kontrol deh segooreedad]
sick bag	bolsa para vómitos [bolssa para bomeetoss]
steward/stewardess	el/la auxiliar de vuelo/la azafata (Am: aeromozo/a) [el/la owksseel-yar deh bwelo/la athafata (ai-romosso/a)]
stopover	escala [esskala]
time of arrival	hora de llegada [ora deh yegada]
timetable	horario (de vuelo) [orar-yo (deh bwelo)]
window seat	asiento junto a la/de ventanilla [assyento khoonto a la/deh bentanee-ya]

TRAVELLING BY TRAIN

AT THE STATION |
EN LA ESTACIÓN DE FERROCARRIL [en la esstath-yon deh ferokareel]

When's the next train to...?	¿Cuándo sale el próximo tren para …? [kwando saleh el proksseemo tren para]
A second-class/first-class single to..., please.	Un billete (Am: boleto) de segunda/de primera clase para …, por favor. [oon bee-yeteh (boleto) deh segoonda/deh preemera klasseh para …, por fabor]
Two returns to..., please.	Dos billetes (Am: boletos) de ida y vuelta a … por favor. [doss bee-yetess (boletoss) deh eeda ee bwelta a … por fabor]

Is there an economy fare?	¿Existe alguna tarifa (de) ahorro?
	[ek-seessteh algoona tareefa (deh) a-oro]
Is there a reduction for children/students?	¿Hacen ustedes descuento para niños/estudiantes?
	[athen oosstedess desskwento para neenyoss/esstood-yantess]
Do I have to reserve a seat?	¿Tendría que reservar un sitio/asiento?
	[tendree-a keh resserbar oon seet-yo/assyento]
Is the train from... running late?	¿Tiene retraso el tren de …?
	[tyeneh retrasso el tren deh]
(Where) Do I have to change?	¿(Dónde) tengo que hacer transbordo?
	[(dondeh) tengo keh ather tranzbordo]
Which platform/track does the train for... leave from?	¿De qué andén sale el tren para …?
	[deh keh anden saleh el tren para]
Can I take a bicycle?	¿Puedo llevar una bicicleta? [pwedo yebar oona beetheekleta]

Excuse me, is this seat free?	Perdón, ¿está libre este asiento?
	[perdon, essta leebreh essteh assyento]
Does this train stop in...?	¿Para este tren en …? [para essteh tren en]
arrive	llegar [yegar]
compartment	departamento (Am: compartimiento)
	[departamento (kompartee-mee-ento)]
connecting train	el tren de enlace [el tren deh enlatheh]
departure, time of departure	salida [saleeda], hora de salida [ora deh saleeda]
emergency brake	freno de alarma [freno deh alarma]
engaged/taken, free/vacant	ocupado [okoopado], libre [leebreh]
fare	precio del billete [preth-yo del bee-yeteh]
get on (the train), **get out**	subir [soobeer], bajar [bakhar]
half	el billete (Am: boleto) infantil [el bee-yeteh (boleto) eemfanteel]
Internet booking/printout	reserva/compra en internet/copia impresa
	[resserba/kompra en eenternet/kop-ya eempressa]
left-luggage/baggage locker	consigna automática [konsseeg-na owtomateeka]
left-luggage/baggage office	consigna (de equipajes) [konsseeg-na (deh ekeepakhess)]
left-luggage/baggage ticket	el talón (Am: boleto) (de equipajes)
	[el talon (boleto) (deh ekeepakhess)]
luggage/baggage	el equipaje [el ekeepakheh]
main station	la estación central [la esstath-yon thentral]
motorail service	el autotrén [el owtotren]
power socket	toma de corriente [toma deh kor-yenteh]
reduction	descuento [desskwento], la reducción [la redook-thyon]
reservation	reserva [resserba]
restaurant/dining car	el vagón restaurante [el bagon resstowranteh]

return ticket	el billete de ida y vuelta [el bee-yeteh deh eeda ee bwelta]
seat reservation	reserva de asiento [resserba deh assyento]
sleeping car	el coche cama [el kocheh kama]
(station) stop, platform/track	parada [parada], el andén/vía [el anden/bee-a]
supplement	suplemento [sooplemento]
ticket	el billete (Am: boleto) [el bee-yeteh (boleto)]
ticket office	ventanilla (Am: boletería) [bentanee-ya (boleteree-a)]
timetable	horario [orar-yo]
toilet/s	baño [banyo], los servicios [los serbeeth-yos]
train	el ferrocarril [el ferokareel], el tren [el tren]
waiting room	sala de espera [sala deh esspera]
window seat	asiento junto a la ventanilla [assyento khoonto a la bentanee-ya]

TRAVELLING BY BOAT

■ AT THE PORT | EN EL PUERTO [en el pwerto]

When does the next ship leave for...?	¿Cuándo parte el próximo barco para …? [kwando parteh el proksseemo barko para]
How long does the crossing take?	¿Cuánto dura la travesía? [kwanto doora la trabessee-a]
I'd like a ticket to...	Quisiera un pasaje para … [keessyera oon passakheh para]
I'd like a ticket for the trip at... o'clock.	Quisiera un pasaje para la excursión de las … [keessyera oon passakheh para la ekss-koor-syon deh lass]
When do we arrive at...?	¿Cuándo atracamos en …? [kwando atrakamoss en]

■ ON BOARD | A BORDO [a bordo]

Where's the restaurant/ lounge?	¿Dónde está el comedor/el salón? [dondeh essta el komedor/el salon]
I don't feel well.	No me siento bien. [no meh syento byen]
Could you give me something for seasickness, please?	¿Puede usted darme un remedio contra el mareo? [pwedeh oossted darmeh oon remed-yo kontra el marayo]

cabin	cabina [kabeena]
captain	el capitán [el kapeetan], la capitana [la kapeetana]
car ferry	el transbordador (Am: el ferryboat) [el tranzbordador (el feree-boht)]
coast, mainland	costa [kossta], tierra firme [tyera feermeh]
deck	cubierta [koob-yerta]
dock	embarcadero [embarkadero]
life-jacket	chaleco salvavidas [chaleko salbabeedass]

lifebelt	el salvavidas [el salbabeedass]
lifeboat	el bote salvavidas [el boteh salbabeedass]
motorboat	(lancha) motora [(lancha) motora]
on board	a bordo [a bordo]
port	puerto [pwerto]
rowing boat	barca de remos [barka deh remoss],
rough seas	el oleaje [el olay-akheh]
seasick	mareado [maray-ado], mareada [maray-ada]
steamer, steamship	el vapor [el bapor]
Steward	camarero (de barco) [kamarero (deh barko)]
ticket	el billete (Am: boleto) [el bee-yeteh (boleto)]
wave	onda [onda]

PUBLIC TRANSPORT

BUS/UNDERGROUND
EL AUTOBÚS/METRO [el owtobooss/metro]

Excuse me, where's the nearest...	Por favor, ¿dónde está la próxima … [por fabor, dondeh essta la proksseema]
bus stop?	parada del autobús? [parada del owtobooss]
tram stop?	parada del tranvía? [parada del trambee-a]
underground station?	parada/estación del metro? [parada/esstath-yon del metro]
Which line goes to..., please?	¿Cuál es la línea que va a …, por favor? [kwal ess la leenaya keh ba a …, por fabor]
Where does the bus leave?	¿Cuándo sale el autobús? [kwando saleh el owtobooss]
Where do I have to get out/change?	¿Dónde tengo que bajar/cambiar? [dondeh tengo keh bakhar/kamb-yar]
Will you tell me when I have to get off, please?	¿Haga el favor de avisarme cuándo tenga que bajar? [aga el fabor deh abeessarmeh kwando tenga keh bakhar]
Where can I buy a ticket?	¿Dónde puedo comprar el billete (Am: boleto)? [dondeh pwedo komprar el bee-yeteh (boleto)]
A ticket to..., please.	Un billete (Am: boleto) a …, por favor. [oon bee-yeteh (boleto) a …, por fabor]
Can I take a bicycle?	¿Puedo llevar una bicicleta? [pwedo yebar oona beetheekleta]

bus, tram	el autobús [el owtobooss], el tranvía [el trambee-a]
buy a ticket	sacar un billete [sakar oon bee-yeteh]
departure	salida [saleeda], partida [parteeda]
driver	el conductor [el kondooktor]
fare	precio del billete [preth-yo del bee-yeteh]
get on/get out	subir [soobeer]/bajar [bakhar]

one-day travelcard	abono diario [abono dee-ar-yo], el billete válido [el bee-yeteh baleedo]
stop	parada [parada]
street, road	la calle [la ka-yeh]
terminus	la estación final [la esstath-yon feenal]
ticket	el billete (Am: boleto) [el bee-yeteh (boleto)]
ticket machine	máquina expendedora de billetes (Am: boletos) [makeena ek-spendedora deh bee-yetess (boletoss)]
timetable	horario [orar-yo]
tourist ticket	el billete (Am: boleto) especial para turistas [el bee-yeteh (boleto) esspeth-yal para tooreesstass]
underground	metro (Am: subterráneo) [metro (soobteranayo)]
weekly season ticket	el billete/abono semanal [el bee-yeteh/abono semanal]

■ TAXI | EL TAXI [el takssee]

Would you call a taxi for me, please?	¿Puede pedirme un taxi, por favor? [pwedeh pedeermeh oon takssee, por fabor]
Where's the nearest taxi rank?	Perdón, ¿dónde está la parada de taxis más cercana? [perdon, dondeh essta la parada deh taksseess mass therkana]
To the station.	A la estación. [a la esstath-yon]
To the... hotel.	Al hotel … [al otel]
To (name of street)	A la calle … [a la ka-yeh]
How much will it cost to...?	¿Cuánto cuesta hasta …? [kwanto kwessta assta]
That's too much.	Me parece demasiado. [meh paretheh demassyado]
Could you stop here, please?	Pare aquí, por favor. [pareh akee, por fabor]
That's for you.	Para usted. [para oossted]
I'd like a receipt, please.	¿Me puede dar una factura, por favor? [meh pwedeh dar oona faktoora, por fabor]

fare, tip/gratuity	tarifa [tareefa], propina [propeena]
taxi driver	taxista m/f [taksseessta]
taxi rank	parada de taxis [parada deh taksseess]

LIFT SHARING

Are you going to...?	¿Va usted a …? [ba oossted a]
Could you give me a lift to...?	¿Podría llevarme hasta …? [podree-a yebarmeh assta]
I'd like to get out here.	Déjeme aquí, por favor. [dekhemeh akee, por fabor]
Thank you very much for the lift.	Muchas gracias por llevarme. [moochass grath-yass por yebarmeh]

> ## A CULINARY ADVENTURE

Order with ease and tuck in with pleasure – foreign menus
will never be an indecipherable mystery again.

GOING FOR A MEAL | IR A COMER [eer a komer]

Is there... here?	¿Dónde hay por aquí cerca ... [dondeh ai por akee therka]
a good restaurant	un buen restaurante? [oon bwen resstowranteh]
a restaurant serving local specialities	un restaurante típico? [oon resstowranteh teepeeko]
I would like to reserve a table for (four) for this evening, please.	¿Puede reservarnos para esta noche una mesa para (cuatro) personas? [pwedeh resserbarnoss para essta nocheh oona messa para (kwatro) perssonass]
A table for (two/three), please.	Una mesa para (dos/tres) personas, por favor. [oona messa para (doss/tress) perssonass, por fabor]

FOOD &
DRINK

Is this table free?	¿Está libre esta mesa? [essta leebreh essta messa]
Do you have a (non)smoking area?	¿Hay también una zona de (no) fumadores? [ai tam-byen oona thona deh (no) foomadoress]
Where are the toilets, please?	¿Dónde están los servicios, por favor? [dondeh esstan loss serbeeth-yoss, por fabor]
Enjoy your meal!, Cheers!	¡Que aproveche! [keh aprobecheh], ¡Salud! [salood]
The food is/was great!	¡La comida está/ha estado estupenda! [la komeeda essta/a esstado esstoopenda]
I'm full, thank you.	No, gracias, ya estoy satisfecho. [no, grath-yass, ya esstoy sateessfecho]
Do you mind if I smoke?	¿Le molesta que fume? [leh molessta keh foomeh]

ORDERING | PEDIDO [pedeedo]

Waiter, could I have...	Camarero/a (Am: Mozo/a), ... [kamarero/a (mosso/a)]
the menu, please.	la carta (Am: el menú), por favor.
	[la karta (el menoo), por fabor]
the drinks menu, please.	la carta de bebidas (y licores), por favor.
	[la karta deh bebeedass (ee leekoress), por fabor]
the wine list, please.	la carta de vinos, por favor. [la karta deh beenoss, por fabor]
What can you recommend?	¿Qué me recomienda usted? [keh meh rekom-yenda oossted]
I'll have...	Yo tomo ... [yo tomo]
I'm sorry but we've run out of...	O lamento, pero ya no tenemos ...
	[o lamento, pero ya no tenemoss]
I'd like to try a local speciality.	Me gustaría algo típico de la región.
	[meh goosstarce a algo teepeeko deh la rekh-yon]
I'm diabetic/vegetarian/vegan.	Soy diabético/vegetariano/vegano.
	[soy dyabeteeko/bekhetar-yano/begano]
I'm allergic to... eggs/gluten/ dairy products/monosodium glutamate/nuts.	Soy alérgico/a a ... [soy alerkheeko/a a ...] los huevos/al gluten/a los productos lácteos/al glutamato sódico/a las nueces. [loss weboss/al glooten/a loss prodooktoss laktayoss/al glootamato sodeeko/a lass nwethess]
What would you like to drink?	¿Qué desea usted beber (Am: tomar)?
	[keh dessaya oossted beber (tomar)]
A glass of..., please.	Un vaso de ..., por favor. [oon basso deh ..., por fabor]
A bottle of/half a bottle of..., please.	Una botella/Media botella de ..., por favor.
	[oona botaya/med-ya botaya deh ..., por fabor]
Bring us..., please.	Tráiganos ..., por favor. [traiganoss ..., por fabor]

COMPLAINTS | QUEJAS Y RECLAMACIONES [kekhass ee reklamath-yoness]

The food is cold.	La comida está fría. [la komeeda essta free-a]
The meat has not been cooked enough.	La carne no está bien hecha. [la karneh no essta byen echa]
Have you forgotten my...?	¿Se ha olvidado usted de mi ...? [seh a olbeedado oossted deh mee]
I didn't order that.	Yo no he pedido esto. [yo no eh pedeedo essto]
Fetch the manager, please.	Llame al dueño, por favor. [yameh al dwenyo, por fabor]

PAYING | PAGAR [pagar]

Could I have the bill/ check, please?	¡La cuenta, por favor!
	[la kwenta, por fabor]
Everything on one bill/ check, please.	Todo junto, por favor.
	[todo khoonto, por fabor]

Could I have a receipt, please?	¿Me puede dar una factura, por favor? [meh pwedeh dar oona faktoora, por fabor]
Separate bills/checks, please.	Cuentas separadas, por favor. [kwentass separadass, por fabor]
That's for you.	Para usted. [para oossted]
Keep the change.	Está bien así. [essta byen assee]
The food was excellent.	La comida estaba excelente. [la komeeda esstaba ekss-thelenteh]
Thank you very much for the invitation!	¡Muchas gracias por la invitación! [moochass grath-yass por la eembeetath-yon]

LOCAL KNOWLEDGE

Insider Tips

Something for every Appetite

Here's a handy guide to help you find the perfect place to eat out when you're travelling in the Spanish-speaking world:

El café [el kafay] – a café that serves much the same fare as its namesake back at home. Some also sell alcohol.

Un bar [oon bar] is a completely different beast to what you might be used to on your native shores. They aren't just places dedicated to drinking: you'll also find that every bar serves snacks – *tapas* [tapass] – to accompany the usual beers and wines. The tradition of serving food in bars originates from a time when people used to cover their wine glasses with slices of bread to stop flies getting at their tipple (tapar = lit: to cover). From these humble beginnings, *tapas* has expanded to include all sorts of tasty treats today, including olives, nuts, anchovies, and a great deal more besides. In Andalusia, these – usually rather substantial – snacks are often given free with your drinks.

La cafetería [la kafeteree-a] – somewhere you can enjoy drinks of all kinds, typical Spanish snacks *(tapas)*, and light meals. All of these goodies can be consumed at the bar, at a table, or on the terrace.

La taberna [la taberna] (popularly known as a **tasca** [tasska]) is a smaller establishment that primarily serves wine. Other drinks are also available.

El (café-)restaurante [el (kafay-)resstowranteh] – a larger venue where you can enjoy something to eat and drink at lunchtime or in the evening.

El chiringuito [el cheereengeeto] – a bar frequented in the summer months that's located outside – almost always on the beach. Serves drinks and meals (typically fish and seafood).

The Bill/Check, Please

When you've finished eating in a restaurant, say *La cuenta, por favor* [la kwenta, por fabor] "The bill/check, please" when it's time to pay. If you're at the bar, however, say ¿Me cobra? [meh kobra] – "Can you cash up?", or ¿Qué le debo? [keh leh debo] – "What do I owe you?"

boil v	cocer [kother]
bread	el pan [el pan]
breakfast	desayuno [dessa-yoono] **> page 46**
cold, (very) hot (temperature)	frío [free-o], (muy) caliente [(mwee) kal-yenteh]
cook (chef), **cook** v	cocinero/a [kotheenero/a], cocinar [kotheenar]
cup, glass	taza [tatha], vaso [basso]
cutlery	los cubiertos [loss koob-yertoss]
dessert	el postre [el posstreh] **> page 51**
diabetic	diabético [dyabeteeko], diabética [dyabeteeka]
dinner	cena [thena]
dish (of the day)	plato (del día) [plato [del dee-a]]
drink	bebida [bebeeda] **> page 45, 52**
fork, knife, spoon	el tenedor [el tenedor], cuchillo [koochee-yo], cuchara [koochara]
fresh, raw	fresco [fressko], crudo [kroodo], cruda [krooda]
deep-fried/fried, grilled	frito [freeto], a la plancha/parrilla [a la plancha/paree-ya]
garlic	ajo [akho]
gluten-free	libre/s de gluten [leebreh/ess deh glooten]
gravy	salsa [salssa]
hot (spicy)	picante [peekanteh], fuerte [fwerteh]
low-calorie/fat	bajo en calorías/grasas [bakho en kaloree-ass/grassass]
lunch	comida [komeeda], almuerzo [almwertho]
main course	comida principal [komeeda preentheepal]
mustard	mostaza [mosstatha]
napkin	servilleta [serbee-yeta]
oil, vinegar	el aceite [el athay-teh], el vinagre [el beenagreh]
order n	pedido [pedeedo]
plate	plato [plato]
portion, children's portion	la ración [la rath-yon], plato para niños [plato para neenyoss]
rare	a la inglesa [a la eenglessa]
salt, pepper	la sal [la sal], pimienta [peem-yenta]
sauce, seasoning	salsa [salssa], mojo [mokho]
soup	sopa [sopa] **> page 47**
sour, sweet	agrio [agree-o], dulce [dooltheh]
spice	especia [esspeth-ya], condimento [kondeemento]
starter	los entremeses [loss entremesess] **> page 47**
(without) sugar	(sin) azúcar [(seen) athookar]
tip/gratuity	propina [propeena]
toothpick	palillo [palee-yo]
tough	duro [dooro]
vegetarian	vegetariano [bekhetar-yano]
waiter, waitress	camarero [kamarero], camarera [kamarera]
water	(el) agua [(el) agwa]
well-done (meat)	(muy) hecho/hecha [(mwee) ech-o/echa]
wholemeal	grano integral [grano eentegral]

lechuga
[lechooga]

las judías
[lass khoodee-ass]
Am: **los porotos/los frijoles**
[loss porotoss/loss freekholess]

guindilla verde
[geendee-ya berdeh]
Am: **el chile**
[el cheeleh]

pimiento verde
[peem-yento berdeh]

los tomates
[loss tomatess]

pepino
[pepeeno]

coliflor f
[koleeflor]

el brécol
[el brekol]

alcachofa
[alka-chofass]

los champiñones
[loss champeenyoness]

berenjena
[beren-khena]

apio
[ap-yo]

las patatas [lass patatass]
Am: **las papas** [lass papass]

cebolla
[theboya]

ajo
[akho]

jengibre m
[khen-kheebreh]

aguacate m
[agwakateh]

las zanahorias
[lass thana-or-yass]

repollo/berza/la col
[repoyo/bertha/la kol]

puerro
[pwero]

los espárragos
[loss essparagoss]

las lentejas
[lass lentekhass]

calabaza
[kalabatha]

calabacín m
[kalabatheen]

los guisantes
[loss geessantess]
Am: **arvejas** [arbekhass]

los garbanzos
[loss garbanthoss]

las espinacas
[lass esspeenakass]

el maíz
[el ma-eeth]

salvia
[salb-ya]

menta
[menta]

el perejil
[el perekheel]

romero
[romero]

los albaricoques
[loss albareekokess]
Am: **los damascos** [loss damasskoss]

plátano [platano]
Am: **banana** [banana]

piña [peenya]
Am: **ananás** [ananass]

mango
[mango]

las fresas
[lass fressass]
Am: **frutilla** [frootee-ya]

melocotón m [melokoton]
Am: **durazno** [doorathno]

el kiwi
[el kee-wee]

las uvas
[lass oobass]

manzana
[manthana]

pera
[pera]

los arándanos
[loss arandanoss]

las cerezas
[lass therethass]

las grosellas
[lass grossayass]

naranja
[narankha]

el limón
[el leemon]

lima
[leema]

papaya
[papa-ya]

sandía
[sandee-a]

el melón
[el melon]

pomelo
[pomelo]

granada
[granada]

las ciruelas
[lass theer-welass]

las ciruelas amarillas
[lass theer-welass amaree-yass]

los higos
[loss eegoss]

el litchi
[el leetchee]

pamplemusa
[pamplemoossa]

coco
[koko]

las castañas
[lass kasstanyass]

los cacahuetes
[loss kaka-wetess]

los arándanos (rojos/agrios)
[loss arandanoss
(rokhoss/agree-oss)]

las frutas desecadas
[lass frootass dessekadass]

surtido de frutos secos
[soorteedo deh frootoss sekoss]

el pan/tostada
[el pan/tosstada]

el pan integral
[el pan eentegral]

barra de pan
[bara deh pan]

el baguette
[el ba-get]

el bagel
[el bakhel]

el brezel/rosquilla (salada)
[el brethel/rosskee-ya (salada)]

el croissant
[el krwa-ssant]

**tostada(s) sueca(s)/pan/
tostada(s) Wasa**
[tosstada(ss) sweka(ss),
pan/tosstada(ss) wassa]

el pan ácimo
[el pan atheemo]

panecillo
[panethee-yo]

panecillo integral
[panethee-yo eentegral]

el pan negro
[el pan negro]

el gofre
[el gofreh]

el donut
[el do-noot]

bollo
[boyo]

torta/tarta
[torta/tarta]

torta de arroz
[torta deh aroth]

el müsli
[el moozlee]

los copos de maíz
[loss koposs deh ma-eeth]

el yogur
[el yogoor]

mantequilla (Am: manteca)
[mantekee-ya (manteka)]

huevo
[we-bo]

queso
[kesso]

el camembert
[el kamember]

queso azul
[kesso athool]

el camembert
[el kamember]

queso fresco
[kesso fressko]

la leche
[la lecheh]

el requesón con hierbas
[el rekesson kon yerbass]

el (queso) Bonbel
[el (kesso) bombel]

(queso) parmesano
[(kesso) parmessano]

queso de oveja
[kesso deh obekha]

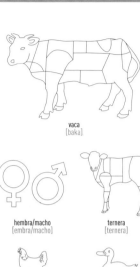

vaca
[baka]

la casquería
[la kasskeree-a]

hembra/macho
[embra/macho]

ternera
[ternera]

cerdo
[therdo]

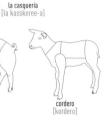

cordero
[kordero]

pollo
[poyo]

pato
[pato]

conejo
[konekho]

el jabalí
[el khabalee]

entera
[entera]

en pedazos m, pl
[en pedathoss]

la carne picada
[la karneh peekada]

pincho de carne
[peencho deh karneh]

el bistec
[el beesstek]

el filete
[el feeleteh]

chuleta [chooleta]
Am: **costeleta** [kossteleta]

el rosbif
[el rozbeef]

salchicha
[salcheecha]

embutido
[embooteedo]

el salami/el salchichón
[el salamee/el salcheechon]

jamón (de) york
[khamon (deh) york]

el jamón serrano
[el khamon serano]

panceta
[pantheta]

pollo asado
[poyo assado]

muslo de pollo
[moozlo deh poyo]

lubina
[loobeena]

trucha
[troocha]

el atún
[el atoon]

el salmón
[el salmon]

las sardinas
[lass sardeenass]

las gambas
[lass gambass]

gambas [gambass]/
camarones [kamaroness]

el bogavante
[el bogabanteh]

los mejillones
[loss mekhee-yoness]

los calamares
[loss kalamaress]

las ostras
[lass osstrass]

el caviar
[el kab-yar]

agua m mineral sin gas
[agwa meeneral seen gass]

agua m mineral con gas
[agwa meeneral kon gass]

la leche
[la lecheh]

la leche de soja
[la lecheh deh sokha]

zumo
[thoomo]

la Coca-Cola
[la koka-kola]

bebida energética
[bebeeda enerkheteeka]

cerveza
[therbetha]

el té
[el teh]

el café
[el kafeh]

cacao
[kak-ow]

los cubitos de hielo
[loss koobeetoss deh yelo]

vino tinto
[beeno teento]

vino blanco
[beeno blanko]

el cava/el champán
[el kaba/el champan]

el cóctel
[el koktel]

> Point & Show: page 43

café solo [kafeh solo]	black coffee
café con leche [kafeh kon lecheh]	coffee with milk
café descafeinado [kafeh desskafaynado]	decaffeinated coffee
té con leche/limón [teh kon lecheh/teemon]	tea with milk/lemon
infusión (de hierbas)/tisana [eemfoossyon (deh yerbass)/teessana]	herbal tea/infusion
chocolate [chokolateh]	hot chocolate
zumo de fruta [thoomo deh froota]	fruit juice
huevo pasado por agua [webo passado por agwa]	soft boiled egg
huevos revueltos [weboss reb-weltoss]	scrambled eggs
huevos con jamón [weboss kon khamon]	eggs with bacon
pan [pan], **panecillos** [panethee-yoss], **tostadas** [tosstadass]	bread, rolls, toast
crema catalana [krema katalana]	crème brûlée: caramelised vanilla pudding
churros [chooross]	long, thin Spanish donuts
mantequilla [mantekee-ya]	butter
queso [kesso]	cheese
embutido [embooteedo]	sausage
jamón (serrano)/(de york) [khamon (serano)/(deh york)]	(raw/cooked) ham
miel [mee-el]	honey
mermelada [mermelada]	jam
müsli [moozlee]	muesli
yogur [yogoor]	yoghurt
fruta [froota]	fruit

ensalada [enssalada]	salad
canelones [kaneloness]	cannelloni: filled, baked rolls of pasta
bacalao al ajillo [bakala-o al akhee-yo]	dried cod with garlic
chuleta de ternera con patatas y guisantes [chooleta deh ternera kon patatass ee geessantess]	veal cutlet with potatoes and peas
gazpacho [gathpacho]	cold soup made from tomatoes, vegetables and spices
pechuga de pollo o merluza [pechooga deh poyo o merlootha]	chicken breast or hake
fruta del tiempo [froota del tyempo]	seasonal fruit

postre (flan o fruta del tiempo) o café
[posstreh (flan o froota del tyempo) o kafeh]

dessert (caramel pudding or seasonal fruit) or coffee

postre: helado, yogurt o tarta de chocolate
[posstreh: elado, yogoort o tarta deh chokolateh]

dessert: ice cream, yoghurt or chocolate tart

ENTREMESES [entremessess] | STARTERS

aceitunas [athaytoonass]	olives
alcachofas [alkachofass]	artichokes
almejas [almekhass]	clams
boquerones [bokeroness]	anchovies
cangrejos [kangrekhoss]	crab
caracoles [karakoless]	snails
chorizo [choreetho]	spicy sausage
croquetas [kroketass]	croquettes
embutido [embooteedo]	sausage
ensaladilla rusa [enssaladee-ya roossa]	potato salad (with vegetables, tuna and mayonnaise)
fiambre [fyambreh]	cold cuts
gambas (al ajillos) [gambass (al akhee-yoss)]	prawns/shrimps (with garlic)
gambas a la plancha [gambass a la plancha]	grilled prawns/shrimps
jamón serrano/(de) york [khamon serano/(deh) york]	raw/cooked ham
mejillones [mekhee-yoness]	mussels
salchichón [salcheechon]	salami
salpicón de marisco [salpeekon deh mareessko]	seafood salad
sardinas [sardeenass]	sardines

SOPAS [sopass] | SOUPS

caldo [kaldo]	broth
consomé [konssomeh]	consommé: clear soup made with rich, flavoursome stock
crema de espárragos [krema deh essparagoss]	cream of asparagus soup
fabada asturiana [fabada asstoor-yana]	bean stew from Asturias
gazpacho [gathpacho]	cold soup made with tomatoes, vegetables and spices
sopa de ajo [sopa deh akho]	garlic and bread soup
sopa de arroz [sopa deh aroth]	rice soup
sopa de fideos [sopa deh feedayoss]	noodle soup
sopa de pescado [sopa deh pesskado]	fish soup
sopa juliana/jardinera/de verduras [sopa khool-yana/khardeenera/deh berdoorass]	vegetable soup

> Point & Show: page 45

anguila [angeela]	eel
angulas [angoolass]	young eels
arenque [arenkeh]	herring
atún [atoon]	tuna
bacalao [bakala-o]	cod/dried cod
besugo [bessoogo]	bream
bogavante [bogabanteh]	lobster
bonito [boneeto]	(young) tuna
caballa [kaba-ya]	mackerel
calamares a la romana [kalamaress a la romana]	squid rings in breadcrumbs
calamares en su tinta [kalamaress en soo teenta]	squid in its own ink
carpa [karpa]	carp
centollo [thentoyo]	spider carb
cigalas [theegalass]	crayfish
corvina [korbeena]	sea bass
dorada [dorada]	gilt-head bream
gambas [gambass]	prawns/shrimps
langosta [langossta]	lobster/crayfish
langostinos [langossteenoss]	king prawns
lenguado [lengwado]	sole
lubina [loobeena]	European sea bass
merluza [merlootha]	hake
paella [pa-aya]	rice dish (with seafood)
parrillada de pescado [paree-yada deh pesskado]	grilled fish platter
perca [perka]	perch
pescadilla [pesskadee-ya]	small hake, whiting
pescado a la marinera [pesskado a la mareenera]	fish cooked "sailor style" (in a tomato and white wine sauce)
pez espada [peth esspada]	swordfish
platija [plateekha]	plaice, flounder
pulpo [poolpo]	octopus
rape [rapeh]	anglerfish
raya [ra-ya]	ray/skate
rodaballo [rodaba-yo]	turbot
salmón [sal-mon]	salmon
salmonete [salmoneteh]	red mullet
trucha [troocha]	trout
zarzuela de marisco(s) [tharthwela deh mareessko(ss)]	seafood casserole

Point & Show: page 44

asado [assado]	roast
bistec [beesstek]	beef steak
cabrito [kabreeto]	kid goat
callos [ka-yoss]	tripe
carne picada [karneh peekada]	mince
cerdo [therdo]	pork
chuleta [chooleta]	cutlet
cocido [kotheedo]	stew (with meat, chickpeas, potatoes and vegetables)
cochinillo [kocheenee-yo]	suckling pig
conejo [konekho]	rabbit
cordero [kordero]	mutton, lamb
cordero lechal [kordero lechal]	(young) lamb
empanada [empanada]	pasty
escalope [esskalopeh]	thin slice of meat (schnitzel)
estofado [esstofado]	pot roast
faisán [faisan]	pheasant
filete [feeleteh]	filet steak, tenderloin
guisado [geessado]	stew, ragout
hígado [eegado]	liver
lengua [lengwa]	tongue
liebre [lee-ebreh]	hare
lomo [lomo]	loin
paella [pa-aya]	rice dish (with seafood)
parrillada de carne [paree-yada deh karneh]	mixed meat grill
pato [pato]	duck
pavo [pabo]	turkey
pechuga de pollo [pechooga deh poyo]	chicken breast
perdiz [perdeeth]	partridge
pichón [peechon]	pigeon
pollo [poyo]	chicken
riñones [reenyoness]	kidneys
rosbif [rozbeef]	roast beef
sesos [sessoss]	brain
solomillo [solomee-yo]	sirloin steak, entrecote steak
ternera [ternera]	calf/veal
vaca [baka]	beef

ENSALADA Y VERDURAS [enssalada ee berdoorass]
SALAD AND VEGETABLES

acelgas [athelgass]	chard
aguacate [agwakateh]	avocado
alcachofas [alkachofass]	artichokes
berenjenas [beren-khenass]	aubergines
cebollas [theboyass]	onions
col de Bruselas [kol deh broosselass]	Brussels sprouts
coliflor [koleeflor]	cauliflower
ensalada variada/mixta [enssalada bar-yada/meekssta]	mixed salad
ensalada del tiempo [enssalada del tyempo]	seasonal salad
escarola [esskarola]	endive
espárragos [essparagoss]	asparagus
frijoles [freekholess]	beans
garbanzos [garbanthoss]	chickpeas
guisantes [geessantess]	peas
judías blancas (alubias) [khoodee-ass blankass (aloobee-ass)]	white beans
judías verdes [khoodee-ass berdess]	green beans
lechuga [lechooga]	lettuce
lentejas [lentekhass]	lentils
patatas [patatass], **papas fritas** [papass freetass]	potatoes, chips/fries
pepino [pepeeno]	cucumber
pimiento [peem-yento]	bell pepper
pisto (manchego) [peessto (manchego)]	stewed vegetable dish
setas [setass]	mushrooms
tomate [tomateh]	tomato
zanahorias [thana-or-yass]	carrots

PLATOS DE HUEVOS [platoss deh weboss] | EGG DISHES

huevos al plato [weboss al plato]	baked eggs (baked in a flat dish)
huevos duros [weboss dooross]	hard-boiled eggs
huevos fritos [weboss freetoss]	fried eggs
huevos pasados por agua [weboss passadoss por agwa]	soft-boiled eggs
huevos revueltos [weboss rebweltoss]	scrambled eggs
tortilla (a la) española [tortee-ya (a la) esspanyola]	Spanish potato omelette
tortilla (a la) francesa [tortee-ya (a la) franthessa]	egg omelette

POSTRES, QUESO Y FRUTA [posstress, kesso ee froota]
DESSERTS, CHEESE AND FRUIT

 Point & Show: page 42, 43

albaricoques [albareekokess]	apricots
arroz con leche [aroth kon lecheh]	rice pudding
cerezas [therethass]	cherries
ciruelas [theer-welass]	plums
compota [kompota]	compote
flan [flan]	crème caramel
fresas [fressass]	strawberries
higos [eegoss]	figs
macedonia (de frutas) [mathedonya (deh frootass)]	fruit salad
mandarina [mandareena]	tangerine
manzana [manthana]	apple
melocotón [melokoton]	peach
melón [melon]	melon
naranja [narankha]	orange
natillas [natee-yass]	custard
pera [pera]	pear
piña [peenya]	pineapple
plátano [platano], **banana** [banana]	banana
pomelo [pomelo], **toronja** [toronkha]	grapefruit
queso de cabra [kesso deh kabra]	goat's cheese
queso de Gruyère [kesso deh grai-yer]	gruyère cheese (firm, tangy cheese)
queso manchego [kesso manchego]	mature sheep's cheese from La Mancha region
queso de oveja [kesso deh obekha]	sheep's cheese
sandía [sandee-a]	watermelon
tarta [tarta]	gateau/tart
uvas [oobass]	grapes

HELADOS [eladoss] | ICE CREAM

café helado [kafeh elado]	iced coffee
copa de helado con frutas [kopa deh elado kon frootass]	ice cream sundae with fruit
helado de chocolate [elado deh chokolateh]	chocolate ice cream
helado de limón [elado deh leemon]	lemon ice cream
helado de vainilla [elado deh bai-nee-ya]	vanilla ice cream
helado variado [elado bar-yado]	assorted ice cream
sorbete [sorbeteh]	sorbet

DULCES [doolthess] | SWEETS

bombón [bombon]   chocolates/pralines
chocolate [chokolateh]   chocolate
churros [chooross]   long, thin Spanish donuts
galletas [ga-yetass]   biscuits/cookies
nata (batida/montada) [nata (bateeda/montada)] (whipped) cream
pastas [passtass], **pasteles** [passteless]   cakes, pastries
pastel [passtel]   cake
pastelitos de crema [passteleetoss deh krema] cream cake
tarta helada [tarta elada]   ice cream tart
tarta de frutas [tarta deh frootass]   fruit flan
tarta de manzana [tarta deh manthana]   apple tart
torta [torta], **tarta** [tarta]   gateau/tart

BEBIDAS NO ALCOHÓLICAS [bebeedass no alko-oleekass] NON-ALCOHOLIC DRINKS

agua mineral [agwa meeneral]   mineral water
batido [bateedo]   milkshake
cacao [kaka-o]   cocoa
(café) americano [(kafeh) amereekano]   large black coffee
café solo [kafeh solo]   espresso
café con leche [kafeh kon lecheh]   milky coffee
(café) cortado [(kafeh) kortado]   espresso with a little milk
(café) descafeinado [(kafeh) desskafaynado]   decaffeinated coffee
horchata [orchata]   almond milk drink
naranjada [narankhada]   orangeade
zumo de fruta [thoomo deh froota]   fruit juice
zumo de limón [thoomo deh leemon]   lemon juice
zumo de naranja [thoomo deh narankha]   orange juice

ALGUNOS VINOS TÍPICOS ESPAÑOLES [algoonoss beenoss teepeekoss esspanyoless] SOME TYPICAL SPANISH WINES

Cariñena [kareenyena]   dry dinner wine
Chacolí [chakolee], **Montilla** [montee-ya]   dry aperitif
Jerez (dulce/oloroso) [khereth (dooltheh/olorosso)] (sweet) sherry
Málaga [malaga]   very sweet dessert wine
Manzanilla [manthanee-ya], **Moriles** [moreeless] dry white wine
Moscatel [mosskatel]   (sweet) dessert wine
Priorato [pree-orato]   red or white wine from Catalonia

THE DRINKS MENU

Ribeiro [reebayro] — red wine from Galicia
Rioja [ree-okha] — red or white wine from La Rioja
Sangría [sangree-a] — mix of red wine, fruit, lemonade and brandy
Valdepeñas [baldepenyass] — red or white wine from La Mancha

OTRAS BEBIDAS ALCOHÓLICAS [otrass bebeedass alko-oleekass]
OTHER ALCOHOLIC DRINKS

aguardiente [agward-yenteh] — liqueur
caña de cerveza [kanya deh therbetha] — a glass of draught beer
champán [champan]**, cava** [kaba] — champagne, bubbly
coñac [konyak] — cognac
Cuba Libre [kooba leebreh] — rum and cola
ginebra [geenebra] — gin
sidra [seedra] — cider

LOCAL KNOWLEDGE

Insider Tips

Your Better Half

If someone in Spain asks you about your *media naranja* [med-ya narankha] ("half an orange"), they haven't gone bananas – they're enquiring about your 'better half'...

¿Te gusta? [meh goosstass]

The Spanish verb *gustar* [goosstar] is a real workhorse of a word. As well as being used to ask if someone's enjoying their meal, the question *¿Te gusta?* [teh goossta] can also be used to ask if you like a person romantically. *¡Me gustas!* [meh goosstass] – "I like/fancy/want/love you!" – is also a good bet for passionate declarations.

Breakfast Blues

If you love tucking into a hearty breakfast, you won't have too much luck in Spanish bars. The most flamboyant fare a normal Spanish breakfast has to offer is a milky coffee with a croissant. If you're looking for something more substantial, you could also order a *bocadillo* [bokadee-yo] – a baguette filled with your choice of Spanish ham, cheese, chorizo and other specialities.

If you've got a sweet tooth in the morning, *Churrerías* [choorer-ee-ass] and some *cafeterías* [kafatereeass] also serve *chocolate conchurros* [chokolateh conchooross]: long, thin Spanish donuts served with thick hot chocolate.

see the menu, page 46

> SUCCESSFUL SHOPPING

Whether you're after chic shoes, the perfect souvenir, a toothbrush or some wholemeal bread, we've equipped you for every eventuality. We've also provided some very handy 'point & show' pictures.

■ AT THE SHOPS | EN LA TIENDA [en la tyenda]

Thanks. I'm just looking around.	Gracias, estoy mirando nada más. [grath-yass, esstoy meerando nada mass]
Excuse me, where can I find...?	Perdone, por favor, ¿dónde hay …? [perdoneh, por fabor, dondeh ai]
I'd like...	Quisiera …/Desearía … [keessyera/dessayaree-a]
Have you got...?	¿Tiene usted …? [tyeneh oossted]
Do you take credit cards?	¿Aceptan ustedes tarjetas de crédito? [atheptan oosstedess tarkhetass deh kredeeto]
How much is it?	¿Cuánto cuesta? [kwanto kwessta]

SHOPPING

That's expensive.	¡Qué caro! [keh karo]
Is there any chance of a discount?	¿Puede hacerme un descuento? [pwedeh athermeh oon desskwento]
The maximum I'm prepared to pay is...	Pagaría un máximo de … [pagaree-a oon maksseemo deh]
I'll take it.	Me lo llevo. [meh lo yebo]
Can you recommend a... shop?	¿Puede usted indicarme una buena tienda de …? [pwedeh oossted eendeekarmeh oona bwena tyenda deh]

OPENING HOURS HORARIO [orar-yo]

open, closed	abierto [ab-yerto], cerrado [therado]

información f turística
[eemformath-yon tooreessteeka]

oficina de correos
[ofeetheena deh korayoss]

farmacia
[farmath-ya]

droguería
[drogeree-a]

panadería
[panaderee-a]

carnicería
[karneetheree-a]

zapatería
[thapateree-a]

óptico
[opteeko]

joyero
[khoyero]

tienda de móviles
[tyenda deh mobeeless]

librería
[leebreree-a]

tienda de discos
[tyenda deh deesskoss]

floristería
[floreessteree-a]

peluquería
[pelookeree-a]

artículos domésticos
[arteekooloss domessteekoss]

agencia de viajes
[akhenth-ya deh bee-akhess]

estanco [Am: cigarrería]
[esstanko [seegar-er-ee-a]]

tienda de informática
[tyenda deh eemformateeka]

frutería y verdulería
[frooteree-a ee berdooleree-a]

tienda macrobiótica
[tyenda makro-bee-oteeka]

el vendedor de periódicos
[el ben-de-dor deh
per-yodee-koss]

juguetería/tienda de)
artículos de juguete
[khoogeteree-a/(tyenda deh)
arteekooloss deh khoogeteh]

(el almacén de) vinos/
la bodega
[(el almathen deh) beenoss/la
bodega]

(tienda de) artículos
de piel/cuero
[(tyenda deh) arteekooloss
deh pyel/kwero]

(tienda de) artículos
eléctricos
[(tyenda deh) arteekooloss
elektreekoss]

(tienda de) artículos
de deporte
[(tyenda deh) arteekooloss
deh deporteh]

(tienda de) artículos
fotográficos
[(tyenda deh) arteekooloss
fotografeekoss]

(tienda de) bebidas alcohólicas,
vinos y licores
[(tyenda deh) bebeedass alko-
oleekass, beenoss ee leekoress]

patisserie (shop selling cakes and pastries)	pastelería [passteleree-a]
department store	los grandes almacenes [loss grandess almatheness]
market, flea market	mercado [merkado], rastro [rasstro]
shopping centre/mall	centro comercial [thentro komerth-yal]

| souvenir shop | tienda de recuerdos [tyenda deh rekwerdoss] |
| supermarket | supermercado [soopermerkado] |

■ THE PHARMACY | FARMACIA [farmath-ya] ■

> At the Doctor's: page 107

| Where's the nearest pharmacy? | ¿Dónde está la farmacia más cercana, por favor? [dondeh essta la farmath-ya mass therkana, por fabor] |
| Can you give me something for... | ¿Me puede dar algo contra ..., por favor? [meh pwedeh dar algo kontra ..., por fabor] |

TAKE... TOME ... [tomeh]

internally/externally	para uso interno/externo [para oosso eenterno/ekssterno]
on an empty stomach	en ayunas [en a-yoonass]
after/before meals	después/antes de las comidas [desspwess/anteh deh lass komeedass]
let it dissolve in your mouth	dejar deshacerse en la boca [dekhar dess-athersseh en la boka]

> Further information: page 60

LOCAL KNOWLEDGE

Insider Tips

Who's Last?

If you're waiting to be served, make sure to secure your place in line by asking *¿Quién es el último?* [kee-en ess el oolteemo] ("who's last").

Sweet Talk

The commonly-heard flirtatious remarks (*piropos* [peeroposs]) that some Spanish men call after passing women shouldn't be taken with offense. *Piropear* should rather be seen as a male pastime, and isn't to be taken too seriously – it's actually more of a competition to see who can come up with the most fantastic phrases than anything else. Don't be surprised to hear *guapo* [gwapo] or *guapa* [gwapa] ("pretty"), *cariño* [kareenyo] ("darling"), *reina* [rayna] ("Queen"), *mi niña* [mee ninya] ("my girl"), *hija* [eekha] ("daughter") or other similar clichés called out in shops, bars and markets. It's not usually an attempt to pick you up, but a sort of common, amicable form of address.

el jabón
[el khabon]

el desodorante
[el dessodoranteh]

crema
[krema]

el papel higiénico
[el papel eekh-yeneeko]

cepillo de dientes
[thepee-yo deh dyentess]

pasta de dientes
[passta deh dyentess]

seda dental
[seda dental]

los pañuelos de papel
[loss pan-yweloss deh papel]

el champú
[el champoo]

el fijador
[el feekhador]

el peine/cepillo del pelo
[el payneh/thepee-yo del pelo]

espejo
[esspekho]

lima de uñas
[leema deh oonyass]

las pinzas
[lass peenthass]

tijera de uñas
[teekhera deh oonyass]

el perfume
[el perfoomeh]

el tampón
[el tampon]

los paños compresa
[loss panyoss kompressa]

el rímel
[el reemel]

el lápiz de labios
[el lapeeth deh lab-yoss]

cuchilla de afeitar
[koochee-ya deh afay-tar]

maquinilla de afeitar
[makeenee-ya deh afay-tar]

la loción
[la loth-yon]

preservativo/el condón
[presserbateebo/el kondon]

crema solar
[krema solar]

botella de agua caliente
[botaya deh agwa kal-yenteh]

esparadrapo
[essparadrapo]

los tapones para los oídos
[loss taponess para loss o-eedoss]

aguja
[agookha]

hilo
[eelo]

los imperdibles
[loss eemper-deebless]

el botón
[el boton]

ELECTRICAL GOODS/COMPUTING/PHOTOGRAPHY
ELECTRÓNICA/INFORMÁTICA/FOTOGRAFÍA

linterna
[leenterna]

bombilla
[bombee-ya]

batería
[bateree-a]

el adaptador
[el adaptador]

el (ordenador) portátil
[el (ordenador) portateel]

cámara fotográfica digital
[kamara fotografeeka deekheetal]

teleobjetivo
[telay-ob-khe-teebo]

batería (recargable)
[bateree-a (rekargableh)]

impresora
[eempressora]

el escáner
[el esskaner]

el (teléfono) móvil
[el (telefono) mobeel]

el cargador (del móvil)
[el kargador (del mobeel)]

el televisor
[el telebeessor]

la radio
[la rad-yo]

el MP3/el iPod
[el emeh-peh-tress/el ai-pod]

los auriculares
[loss owreekoo-laress]

el carrete
[el kareteh]

diapositiva
[dee-a-possee-teeba]

cámara fotográfica sumergible
[kamara fotografeeka
soomer-kheebleh]

cámara de vídeo/filmadora
[kamara deh beedayo/
feelmadora]

el despertador
[el desspertador]

máquina de afeitar
[makeena deh afay-tar]

cepillo de dientes eléctrico
[thepee-yo deh dyentess elektreeko]

el secador de pelo
[el sekador deh pelo]

el cable de la batería
(del portátil)
[el kableh deh la bateree-a
(del portateel)]

el CD/el DVD
[el theh-deh/el
deh-oobeh-deh]

el pen drive/
el stick de memoria
[el pen draif/
el steek deh memor-eea]

tarjeta memoria/
la memory card
[tarkheta memoree-a/
la memoree kard]

antibiotics	antibiótico [antee-bee-oteeko]
antidote	antídoto [anteedoto]
aspirin	aspirina [asspeereena]
(burn) ointment	pomada (para quemaduras) [pomada (para kemadoorass)]
circulatory stimulant	medicamento para la circulación de la sangre [medeekamento para la theerkoolath-yon deh la sangreh]
condom	preservativo [presserbateebo], el condón [el kondon]
contraceptive pill, morning-after pill	píldora anticonceptiva [peeldora anteekonthepteeba], píldora del día después [peeldora del dee-a desspwess]
cough mixture	el jarabe (contra la tos) [el kharabeh (kontra la toss)]
disinfectant	el desinfectante [el desseemfektanteh]
drops	las gotas [lass gotass]
ear drops	las gotas para los oídos [lass gotass para loss o-eedoss]
eye drops	las gotas para los ojos [lass gotass para loss okhoss]
gauze	gasa [gassa]
headache tablets	las pastillas para el dolor de cabeza [lass passtee-yass para el dolor deh kabetha]
insect repellent	el insecticida [el eensek-tee-theeda]
(tincture of) iodine	tintura de yodo [teentoora deh yodo]
laxative	el laxante [el lakssanteh]
medicine	medicina [medeetheena], medicamento [medeekamento]
painkillers	las pastillas contra el dolor [lass passtee-yass kontra el dolor]
prescription	la receta [la retheta]
remedy	remedio [remed-yo]
sedative, tranquilizer	el tranquilizante [el trankeeleethanteh]
side effects	los efectos secundarios [loss efektoss sekoondar-yoss]
sleeping tablets	los somníferos [loss somneefeross]
sticking plasters/ adhesive bandages	esparadrapo [essparadrapo]
stomach pain relief	las gotas para el dolor de estómago [lass gotass para el dolor deh esstomago]
sunburn	quemadura de sol [kemadoora deh sol]
suppositories	los supositorios [loss sooposs-ee-tor-yoss]
tablet/pill	pastilla [passtee-ya], comprimido [kompreemeedo]
thermometer	termómetro [termometro]
throat lozenges	las pastillas para la garganta [lass passtee-yass para la garganta]

■THE HAIRDRESSER'S | PELUQUERÍA [pelookeree-a]

Can I make an appointment for tomorrow?	¿Puede usted darme hora (Am: un turno) para mañana? [pwedeh oossted darmeh ora (oon toorno) para manyana]
Wash and cut/dry cut, please.	Cortar y lavar/Cortar sin lavar, por favor. [kortar ee labar/kortar seen labar, por fabor]

A bit shorter,/ Not too short,/Very short, please.	Un poco más coro,/No demasiado corto,/ Muy corto, por favor. [oon poko mass korto/no demassyado korto/ mwee korto, por fabor]
I'd like a shave, please.	Afeitar, por favor. [afay-tar, por fabor]
Would you trim my beard, please.	Córteme un poco la barba, por favor. [kortemeh oon poko la barba, por fabor]
Thank you. That's fine.	Muchas gracias. Está muy bien así. [moochass grath-yass essta mwee byen assee]
beard, moustache	barba [barba], el bigote [el beegoteh]
blond	rubio [roob-yo]
blow dry v	secar [sekar]
colour/dye v	teñir [ten-yeer]
comb v	peinar [paynar]
curls	los rizos (Am: los rulos) [loss reethoss (loss rooloss)]
cut the ends	cortar las puntas [kortar lass poontass]
dandruff	caspa [kasspa]
do someone's hair	peinar [paynar]
fringe	flequillo [flekee-yo]
hair	pelo [pelo]
haircut, hairstyle	el corte de pelo [el korteh deh pelo], peinado [paynado]
highlights	reflejos [reflekhos], mejas [mekhas]
layers	las capas [lass kapass]
parting	raya [ra-ya]
pluck (your) eyebrows	depilar las cejas [depeelar lass thekhass]
shampoo	el champú [el champoo]
straighten	alisar [aleessar]

■ CLOTHING | ROPA [ropa]

Can you show me...?	¿Puede usted enseñarme …? [pwedeh oossted enssenyarmeh]
Can I try it on?	¿Puedo probármelo? [pwedo probarmelo]
What size do you take?	¿Qué talla tiene usted? [keh ta-ya tyeneh oossted]
It's too small/big.	Me resulta demasiado estrecho, estrecha (Am: angosto, angosta)/anchos, anchas. [meh ressoolta demassyado esstrecho, esstrecha (angossto, angossta)/anchoss, anchass]
It's a good fit. I'll take it.	Me va muy bien. Me lo llevo. [meh ba mwee byen meh lo yebo]
It's not quite what I wanted.	No es exactamente lo que yo quería. [no ess ekssaktamenteh lo keh yo keree-a]
Do you have it in a different colour?	¿Tendría el mismo/la misma en otro color? [tendree-a el meezmo/la meezma en otro kolor]
Thank you, I'll have to think about it.	Gracias, pero me lo tengo que pensar. [grath-yass, pero meh lo tengo keh penssar]

camiseta
[kameesseta]

el jersey (Am: el pulóver)
[el kherssay (el poolober)]

el suéter con capucha
[el sweter kon kapoocha]

chaqueta (Am: saco)
[chaketa (sako)]

el pantalón
[el pantalon]

el pantalón corto
[el pantalon korto]

falda
[falda]

el cinturón
[el theentooron]

blusa
[bloossa]

camisa
[kameessa]

el blázer
[el bla-ther]

chaqueta de punto/rebeca
[chaketa deh poonto/rebeka]
Am: saco tejido [sako tekheedo]

el traje
[el trakheh]

vestido
[bessteedo]

el traje de chaqueta
[el trakheh deh chaketa]

abrigo
[abreego]

los leotardos/el panty
[loss layotardoss/el pantee]

ropa interior
[ropa eenter-yor]

el albornoz
[el albornoth]

los calcetines, las medias
[loss kaltheteeness,
lass med-yass]

el bañador/el pantalón de baño
[el banyador/
el pantalon deh banyo]

el traje de baño
[el trakheh deh banyo]

el bikini
[el beekeenee]

gorra
[gora]

sombrero
[sombrero]

los guantes
[loss gwantess]

el chal/pañuelo de cuello
[el chal/pan-ywelo deh kwayo]

FOOD & DRINK | LOS COMESTIBLES [loss komessteebless]

> You'll find an extensive list of culinary delights in the FOOD & DRINK chapter starting on page 36.

What's that?	¿Qué es esto? [keh ess essto]
Can I try it?	¿Podría probarlo? [podree-a probarlo]
Do you sell...	¿Venden …? [benden]
organic products?	productos biológicos [prodooktoss bee-olo-kheekoss]
local products?	productos de la región [prodooktoss deh la rekh-yon]
I'd like...	Deme …, por favor. [demeh …, por fabor]
a pound (500 g)...,	medio kilo de … [med-yo keelo deh]
a kilo of...	un kilo de … [oon keelo deh]
a piece of...	un trozo de … [oon trotho deh]
a packet of...	un paquete de … [oon paketeh deh]
a tin of...	un bote de … [oon boteh de]
a bottle of...	una botella de … [oona botaya deh]
a bag, please.	una bolsa [oona bolssa]
Thanks, that's everything.	Eso es todo, gracias. [esso ess todo, grath-yass]

beer	cerveza [therbetha] > page 45, 53
beverages/drinks	las bebidas [lass bebeedass] > page 45, 52
bread	el pan [el pan] > page 43, 46
butter	mantequilla (Am: manteca) [mantekee-ya (manteka)] > page 43, 46
cake, gateau/tart	el pastel [el passtel], la tarta [la tarta] > page 43, 52
cheese	queso [kesso] > page 43, 46, 51
chicken	pollo [poyo] > page 44
chocolate	el chocolate [el chokolateh]
chocolate bar	barra/barrita de chocolate [bara/bareeta deh chokolateh]
coffee	el café [el kafeh] > page 45, 52
cold cuts	el embutido [el embooteedo], los fiambres variados [loss fyambress bar-yadoss]
cookies/biscuits	las galletas [lass ga-yetass], pastas [passtass]
cream	crema [krema], nata [nata]
dairy products	productos lácteos [prodooktoss laktayoss] > page 43, 46
eggs	los huevos [loss weboss] > page 43, 46
fish	pescado [pesskado] > page 45, 48
flour	harina [areena]
fresh	fresco [fressko]
fruit	fruta [froota] > page 42, 46, 51
garlic	ajo [akho]
ice cream	helado [elado] > page 47

jam	mermelada [mermelada] > page 46
margarine	margarina [margareena]
mayonnaise	mayonesa [ma-yon-essa]
meat	la carne [la karneh] > page 44, 49
milk	la leche [la lecheh] > page 43, 46
mineral water	(el) agua mineral [(el) agwa meeneral] > page 45, 52
mustard	mostaza [mosstatha]
non-alcoholic beer	cerveza sin alcohol [therbetha seen alko-ol]
noodles	la pasta [la passta]
nuts	los frutos secos [loss frootoss sekoss] > page 43
oil	el aceite [el athay-teh]
orange juice	zumo de naranja [thoomo deh narankha] > page 52
organic food	comida orgánica [komeeda organeeka]
pastries	las pastas [lass passtass],
	las galletas [lass ga-yetass] > page 43, 52
patisserie	pastelería [passteleree-a]
(cakes and pastries)	> page 43, 46, 52
pepper	pimienta [peem-yenta]
poultry	aves [abess] > page 44, 49
(without) preservatives	(sin) conservantes [(seen) konsserbantess]
preserves/tinned food	las conservas [lass konsserbass]
salad	ensalada [enssalada] > page 41, 50
salt	la sal [la sal]
sausage	salchicha [salcheecha]
sausage	embutido [embooteedo] > page 44
skimmed milk	la leche semidesnatada
	[la lecheh semee-dez-natada]
soda/pop	limonada [leemonada]
soup	sopa [sopa] > page 47
spices	especias [esspeth-yass]
(without) sugar	(sin) azúcar [(seen) athookar]
sweets	los dulces [loss doolthess],
	las golosinas [lass golosseenass] > page 52
tea	el té [el teh] > page 43, 45
tea bag	bolsita de té [bolsseeta deh teh]
toast	tostada [tosstada] > page 45, 46
vegetables	las verduras [lass berdoorass] > page 41, 50;
	(pulses/legumes) las legumbres [lass legoombress]
vinegar	el vinagre [el beenagreh]
wholemeal	integral [eentegral]
wine	vino [beeno] > page 52
yoghurt	el yogur [el yogoor] > page 43, 46

■ THE OPTICIAN'S | ÓPTICO [opteeko] ■■■■■■■■

Could you repair these glasses for me, please?	¿Puede usted arreglarme estas gafas (Am: estos anteojos/lentes), por favor? [pwedeh oossted areglarmeh esstass gafass (esstoss antay-okhoss/lentess), por fabor]
I'm short-sighted/ long-sighted.	Soy miope/hipermétrope. [soy mee-opeh/eepermetropeh]
What's your prescription?	¿Cuál es su agudeza visual? [kwal ess soo agoodetha beesswal]
in the right eye,	a la derecha [a la derecha],
in the left eye	a la izquierda [a la eeth-kyerda]
I need some...	Necesito … [nethesseeto]
soaking solution	líquido para conservar lentillas [leekeedo para konsserbar lentee-yass]
cleansing solution	liquido para limpiar lentillas [leekeedo para leemp-yar lentee-yass]
for hard/soft contact lenses.	para lentes de contacto duras/blandas. [para lentess deh kontakto doorass/blandass]
I'm looking for...	Quisiera … [keessyera]
daily disposable lenses.	lentillas (Am: lentes) de un día. [lentee-yass (lentess) deh oon dee-a]
some sunglasses.	unas gafas de sol. [oonass gafass deh sol]
some binoculars.	unos prismáticos. [oonoss preezmateekoss]

■ THE JEWELLER'S | JOYAS Y BISUTERÍA [khoyass ee beessooteree-a] ■■■■■

My watch doesn't work. Could you have a look at it?	Mi reloj no funciona. ¿Puede usted mirar lo que tiene? [mee relokh no foonth-yona pwedeh oossted meerar lo keh tyeneh]
I'd like a nice souvenir/ present.	Busco un recuerdo/regalo bonito. [boossko oon rekwerdo/regalo boneeto]

bracelet	pulsera [poolssera], el brazalete [el brathaleteh]
brooch	el broche [el brocheh]
costume jewellery	bisutería [beessooteree-a]
crystal	el cristal (de roca) [el kreesstal (deh roka)]
earrings	los pendientes (Am: los aretes) [loss pend-yentess (loss aretess)]
genuine	legítimo [lekheeteemo]
gold, silver	oro [oro], plata [plata]
jewellery	las joyas [lass khoyass]
necklace	el collar [el koyar], cadena [kadena]
pearl	perla [perla]
pendant	el colgante [el kolganteh]
ring	anillo [anee-yo]
(precious) stone	piedra (preciosa) [pyedra (preth-yossa)]

waterproof	resistente al agua [resseesstenteh al agwa]
wristwatch	el reloj de pulsera [el relokh deh poolssera]

■ THE SHOE SHOP | ZAPATERÍA [thapateree-a]

I'd like a pair of... shoes.	Quiero un par de zapatos ... [kyero oon par deh thapatoss]
I take a size...	Calzo el número ... [kaltho el noomero]
They're too small/big.	Son demasiado estrechos, estrechas/anchos, anchas. [son demassyado esstrechoss, esstrechass/anchoss, anchass]

boots	las botas [lass botass]
(with) heels	(con) tacón [(kon) takon]
hiking boots	botas de monte/de trekking [botass deh monteh/deh trekeeng]
ladies' shoes	zapato de mujer [thapatoss deh mookher]
leather/rubber sole	suela de cuero/goma [swela deh kwero/goma]
men's shoes	zapatos de caballero [thapatoss deh kaba-yero]
moccasins	mocasines m [el mokasseeness]
wellies, rubber/gum boots	las botas de goma [lass botass deh goma]
sandals	las sandalias [lass sandal-yass]
shoe polish	el betún [el betoon]
shoes	los zapatos [loss thapatoss]
trainers	las zapatillas de deporte [lass thapatee-yass deh deporteh]

■ SOUVENIRS | RECUERDOS [rekwerdoss]

I'd like...	Quisiera ... [keessyera]
a nice souvenir.	un recuerdo bonito. [oon rekwerdo boneeto]
something that's typical of this region.	algo típico de esta zona. [algo teepeeko deh essta thona]
I'd like something that's not too expensive.	Quisiera algo que no sea demasiado caro. [keessyera algo keh no saya demassyado karo]
That's lovely.	Esto es muy bonito. [essto ess mwee boneeto]
Can you gift wrap it for me, please?	¿Podría envolvérmelo/a para regalo? [podree-a embolbermelo/a para regalo]
Thanks, but I didn't find anything (I liked).	Gracias, pero no veo nada que me guste. [grath-yass, pero no bayo nada keh meh goossteh]

ceramics	cerámica [therameeka]
genuine	auténtico [owtenteeko]
hand-made	hecho a mano [echo a mano]
jewellery	las joyas [lass khoyass]
local products,	los productos tradicionales/típicos
local specialities	[loss prodooktoss tradeeth-yonaless/teepeekoss]
pottery	los objetos de cerámica
	[loss obkhetoss deh therameeka]
souvenir	recuerdo [rekwerdo]
textiles	los tejidos [loss tekheedoss]
wood sculptures/carvings	tallas de madera [ta-yass deh madera]

■STATIONERY AND BOOKS | PAPELERÍA Y LIBROS [papeleree-a ee leebross] ■■

I'd like...	Quisiera ... [keessyera]
an English newspaper.	un periódico inglés. [oon per-yodeeko eengless]
a magazine.	una revista. [oona rebeessta]
a travel guide.	una guía turística. [oona gee-a tooreessteeka]
a novel in English.	una novela en inglés. [oona nobela en eengless]
a detective novel.	una novela policíaca. [oona nobela poleethee-aka]
ballpoint pen/biro	bolígrafo (Am: lapicero de bolilla)
	[boleegrafo (lapeessero deh bolee-ya)]
cookbook	libro de cocina [leebro deh kotheena]
envelope	el sobre [el sobreh]
eraser	goma de borrar [goma deh borar]
glue	la goma [la goma], pegamanto [pegamanto]
hiking map of the area	un mapa de senderismo de esta zona
	[oon mapa deh sendereezmo deh essta thona]
magazine	revista [rebeessta]
map	el mapa [el mapa]
newspaper	periódico [per-yodeeko]
notepad	el bloc [el blok]/
	la libreta de apuntes [la leebreta deh apoontess]
novel	novela [nobela]
paper	el papel [el papel]
pencil	el lápiz [el lapeeth], lapicero [lapeethero]
postcard	la postal [la posstal]
sketchbook	el bloc/el cuaderno de dibujo
	[el blok/el kwaderno deh deebookho]
stamp	sello (Am: estampilla) [sayo (esstampee-ya)]
town map	plano de la ciudad [plano deh la th-yoodad]
writing/letter paper	el papel de escribir [el papel deh esskreebeer]

>A ROOM WITH A VIEW

Service with a smile: whether you want to pay a bill by credit card,
access your hotel's Wi-Fi or get childcare at a holiday resort –
all you have to do is ask!

GENERAL INFORMATION

 Planning Your Trip: page 6

Can you recommend..., please?	Perdón, ¿Podría usted recomendarme … [perdon, podree-a oossted rekomendarmeh]
a hotel, a guesthouse	un hotel?, una pensión? [oon otel/oona penssyon]
a campsite	un camping? [oon kampeeng]
Can you recommend anywhere nearby?	¿Podría recomendarme algo por aquí/acá cerca? [podree-a rekomendarmeh algo por akee/aka therka]

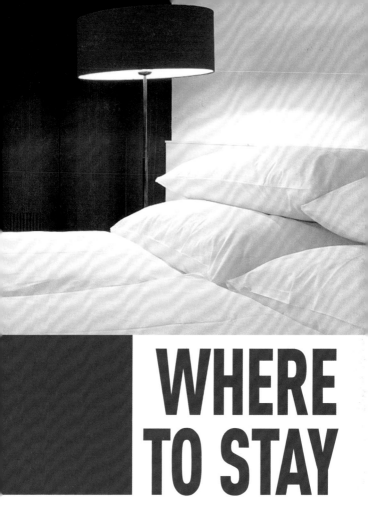

WHERE TO STAY

AT A HOTEL

■ RECEPTION DESK | RECEPCIÓN [rethepth-yon] ■

I've reserved a room.	He reservado una habitación. [eh resserbado oona abeetath-yon]
My name is...	Me llamo … [meh yamo]
Have you got any vacancies...	¿Tienen ustedes habitaciones libres … [tyenen oosstedess abeetath-yoness leebress]
...for one night?/...for two days?/...for a week?	… para una noche? [para oona nocheh]/… para dos días? [para doss dee-ass]/ … para una semana? [para oona semana]

No, I'm afraid we're full.	Lo siento, está todo ocupado. [lo syento, essta todo okoopado]
Yes, what sort of room would you like?	Sí. ¿Qué clase de habitación desea usted? [see keh klasseh deh abeetath-yon dessaya oossted]
a single room	una habitación individual [oona abeetath-yon eendeebeedoo-al]
a double room	una habitación doble [oona abeetath-yon dobleh]
with a shower	con ducha [kon doocha]
with a bath	con baño [kon banyo]
a quiet room	una habitación tranquila [oona abeetath-yon trankeela]
with a view of the sea	con vista(s) al mar [kon beessta(ss) al mar]
Can I see the room?	¿Podría ver la habitación? [podree-a ber la abeetath-yon]
Can you put another bed in the room?	¿Pueden ustedes poner una cama? [pweden oosstedess poner oona kama]
Do you have Wi-Fi?	¿Tienen (conexión) wifi? [tyenen (konekssyon) wai-fai]
How much is the room with...	¿Cuánto cuesta la habitación con … [kwanto kwessta la abeetath-yon kon]
breakfast?	desayuno? [dessa-yoono]
breakfast and an evening meal (half board)?	media pensión? [med-ya penssyon]
full board?	pensión completa? [penssyon kompleta]
What time is breakfast?	¿Desde qué hora se puede desayunar? [dezdeh keh ora seh pwedeh dessa-yoonar]
Where's the restaurant?	¿Dónde está el restaurante? [dondeh essta el resstowranteh]
Please wake me at... o'clock in the morning.	Haga el favor de despertarme mañana a las … [aga el fabor deh desspertarmeh manyana a lass]
Can I have my key, please?	Mi llave, por favor. [mee yabeh, por fabor]

 Breakfast: FOOD & DRINK, page 46

■COMPLAINTS | RECLAMACIONES [reklamath-yoness]

The room hasn't been cleaned.	La habitación no está limpia. [la abeetath-yon no essta leemp-ya]
The shower...	La ducha … [la doocha]
The toilet cistern/tank...	La cisterna/descarga de agua … [la theess-terna/desskarga deh agwa]
The heating...	La calefacción … [la kalefak-thyon]
The light...	La luz … [la looth]
...doesn't work.	… no funciona. [no foonth-yona]
There's no (warm) water.	No sale agua (caliente). [no saleh agwa (kal-yenteh)]
The toilet/washbasin is blocked.	El baño/El lavabo está atascado (Am: tapado). [el banyo/el lababo essta atasskado (tapado)]

What time do I have to check out by?	¿A qué hora tengo que dejar la habitación? [a keh ora tengo keh dekhar la abeetath-yon]
Can I leave my luggage/ baggage here (until this evening), please?	¿Podría dejar aquí mi equipaje (hasta esta tarde/noche)? [podree-a dekhar akee mee ekee-pakheh (assta essta tardeh/nocheh)]
I'm leaving this evening/ tomorrow at... o'clock.	Me marcho esta tarde/mañana a las … [meh marcho essta tardeh/manyana a lass]
Can I have the bill/check, please.	Prepáreme la cuenta, por favor. [preparemeh la kwenta, por fabor]
Can I pay by credit card?	¿Aceptan ustedes tarjetas de crédito? [atheptan oosstedess tarkhetass deh kredeeto]
Thank you very much for everything. Goodbye!	Muchas gracias por todo. ¡Adiós! [moochass grath-yass por todo ad-yoss]
adapter	el adaptador [el adaptador]
air conditioning	el aire acondicionado [el ai-reh akondeeth-yonado]
baby monitor	el intercomunicador (para bebés) [el eenterkomooneekador (para bebess)], el vigilabebés [el beekheela-bebess]
babysitting service	guardería infantil [gwarderee-a eemfanteel]
bathrobe/dressing gown	el albornoz [el albornoth]
bathroom	cuarto de baño [kwarto deh banyo]

LOCAL KNOWLEDGE

Insider Tip

The Perfect Place to Stay

As well as using the usual star ratings, Spanish accommodation is classified with a system of letters that you'll see emblazoned on the signs hung outside. "H" means *hotel* [otel], for instance, while "HR" stands for *Hotel Residencia* [otel resseedenthee-a], a hotel without a restaurant. You also won't usually find a restaurant at a *Hostal* [osstal] or guesthouse – a type of establishment marked out with the letters "HS". Spanish hostels and inns display a "P" (for *Pensión* [penss-yon]) or an "F" (for *Fonda* [fonda]) outside. *Moteles* [moteless] ("motels") proudly display an "M" on their signs, and if you see "PT", you're dealing with a *Parador* [parador] – a comfortable, stylish, state-run hotel, usually located in a historic building (cloisters, forts, castles, etc.). Don't rely too heavily on the star-rating system – the number of stars isn't always a reliable indication of quality in Spain. It's much better to take your hints from recommendations and reviews instead.

> The MARCO POLO travel guides to Spain are fantastic when choosing the perfect place to stay. You'll also find great tips at *www.marco-polo.com*.

bed	cama [kama]
bed and breakfast	alojamiento (con desayuno) [alokha-mee-ento (kon dessa-yoono)]
bed linen	ropa de cama [ropa deh kama]
bedside table	mesita de noche [messeeta deh nocheh]
breakfast	desayuno [dessa-yoono]
breakfast room	sala de desayuno [sala deh dessa-yoono]
(chamber)maid	camarera (del hotel) [kamarera (del otel)]
clean v	limpiar [leemp-yar]
cot	cama de niño [kama deh neenyo]
cupboard	armario [armar-yo]
dinner (evening meal)	cena [thena]
dry cleaner's	servicio de tintorería/limpieza [serbeeth-yo deh teentor-er-ee-a/leemp-yetha]
floor (storey)	piso [peesso]
full board	la pensión completa [la penssyon kompleta]
half board	media pensión [med-ya penssyon]
heating	la calefacción [la kalefak-thyon]
high season	temporada alta [temporada alta]
iron n	plancha [plancha]
key	la llave [la yabeh]
lamp	lámpara [lampara]
low season	temporada baja [temporada bakha]
lunch	comida [komeeda], almuerzo [almwertho]
pillow	almohada [almo-ada]
playroom	habitación de juego (para niños) [abeetath-yon deh khwego (para neenyoss)]
plug	clavija de enchufe [klabeekha deh enchoofeh]
porter	portero [portero]
reading lamp	lámpara de mesita de noche [lampara deh messeeta deh nocheh]
reception	la recepción [la rethepth-yon]
reservation	reserva [resserba]
restaurant	el restaurante [el resstowranteh]
room	la habitación (Am: pieza) [la abeetath-yon (pyessa)]
safe	caja fuerte [kakha fwerteh]
shower	ducha [doocha]
socket (electric)	(caja de) el enchufe [(kakha deh) el enchoofeh]
tap/faucet	grifo (Am: canilla) [greefo (kanee-ya)]
toilet paper	el papel higiénico [el papel eekh-yeneeko]
toilets	los servicios [loss serbeeth-yoss], baño [banyo]
towel	toalla [to-a-ya]
washbasin	lavabo [lababo]
(cold/hot) water	el agua (fría/caliente) [el agwa (free-a/kal-yenteh)]
Wi-Fi	el/la wifi [el/la wai-fai]
window	ventana [bentana]

IN A HOLIDAY HOME

 Planning Your Trip: page 6

Is electricity/water included in the price?	¿Está incluido en el alquiler el precio de la electricidad/del agua? [essta eenkloo-eedo en el alkeeler el preth-yo deh la elektreetheedad/del agwa]
Are bed linen and towels provided?	¿Hay ropa de cama y toallas? [ai ropa deh kama ee to-a-yass]
Are pets allowed?	¿Admiten ustedes animales domésticos? [admeeten oosstedess aneemaless domessteekoss]
Where can we pick up the keys to the house/the apartment?	¿Dónde nos entregan las llaves para la casa? [dondeh noss entregan lass yabess para la kassa]
Do we have to clean the apartment before we leave?	¿Tenemos que encargarnos nosotros de la limpieza final? [tenemoss keh enkargarnoss nossotross deh la leemp-yetha feenal]

additional costs	los gastos adicionales [loss gasstoss adeeth-yonaless]
bed linen	ropa de cama [ropa deh kama]
bedroom	dormitorio [dormeetor-yo]
bottle opener	el abrebotellas [el abrebotayass]
corkscrew	el sacacorchos [el sakakorchoss]
day of arrival	el día de llegada [el dee-a deh yegada]
deposit (down payment)	pago anticipado/de garantía [pago anteetheepado/deh garantee-a]
deposit (security)	depósito [deposseeto]
electricity	la corriente [la kor-yenteh], la electricidad [la elektreetheedad]
end-of-stay cleaning	limpieza final [leemp-yetha feenal]
flat/apartment	apartamento (Am: departamento) [apartamento (departamento)]
holiday camp	la urbanización de vacaciones [la oorbaneethath-yon deh bakath-yoness]
holiday flat/apartment	piso (Am: apartamento) de vacaciones [peesso (apartamento) deh bakath-yoness]
holiday home	casa de vacaciones [kassa deh bakath-yoness]
key	la llave [la yabeh]
kitchenette	la minicocina [la meenee-kotheena]
landlord/lady	dueño/dueña de la casa [dwenyo/dwenya deh la kassa]
pets	los animales domésticos [loss aneemaless domessteekoss]
rent n	el alquiler [el alkeeler]
rent v	alquilar [alkeelar]
rubbish/garbage	basura [bassoora]
sofa bed	el sofá cama [el sofa kama]
towel, dishcloth	toalla [to-a-ya], paño de cocina [panyo deh kotheena]
waste sorting/separation	la separación de basuras [la separath-yon deh bassoorass]

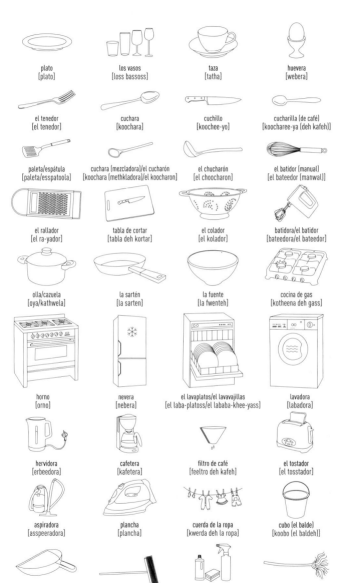

plato
[plato]

los vasos
[loss bassoss]

taza
[tatha]

huevera
[webera]

el tenedor
[el tenedor]

cuchara
[koochara]

cuchillo
[koochee-yo]

cucharilla (de café)
[koocharee-ya (deh kafeh)]

paleta/espátula
[paleta/esspatoola]

cuchara (mezcladora)/el cucharón
[koochara (methkladora/el koocharon]

el chucharón
[el choocharon]

el batidor (manual)
[el bateedor (manwal)]

el rallador
[el ra-yador]

tabla de cortar
[tabla deh kortar]

el colador
[el kolador]

batidora/el batidor
[bateedora/el bateedor]

olla/cazuela
[oya/kathwela]

la sartén
[la sarten]

la fuente
[la fwenteh]

cocina de gas
[kotheena deh gass]

horno
[orno]

nevera
[nebera]

el lavaplatos/el lavavajillas
[el laba-platoss/el lababa-khee-yass]

lavadora
[labadora]

hervidora
[erbeedora]

cafetera
[kafetera]

filtro de café
[feeltro deh kafeh]

el tostador
[el tosstador]

aspiradora
[asspeeradora]

plancha
[plancha]

cuerda de la ropa
[kwerda deh la ropa]

cubo (el balde)
[koobo (el baldeh)]

el recogedor
[el reko-khedor]

escoba
[esskoba]

el detergente/producto de limpieza
[el deterkhenteh/prodookto deh leemp-yetha]

fregona
[fregona]

AT A CAMPSITE

Have you got room for a caravan/tent?
¿Tienen ustedes sitio para una caravana (Am: una casa rodante)/una tienda (Am: una carpa)? [tyenen oosstedess seet-yo para oona karabana (oona kassa rodanteh)/oona tyenda (oona karpa)]

How much does it cost per day and per person?
¿Cuánto cuesta por día y por persona? [kwanto kwessta por dee-a ee por perssona]

What's the price for...
¿Cuánto se paga por ... [kwanto seh paga por]

...a car?
... un coche (Am: un carro)? [oon kocheh (oon karo)]

...a caravan?
... una caravana (Am: una casa rodante)? [oona karabana (oona kassa rodanteh)]

...a mobile home?
... una autocaravana? [oona owtokarabana]

...a tent?
... una tienda (Am: una carpa)? [oona tyenda (oona karpa)]

We'll be staying for... days/weeks.
Pensamos quedarnos ... días/semanas. [penssamoss kedarnoss ... dee-ass/semanass]

Where are...
¿Dónde están ... [dondeh esstan]

the toilets?
los servicios? [loss serbeeth-yoss]

the washrooms?
los lavabos? [loss lababoss]

the showers?
las duchas? [lass doochass]

Are there any electric hook-up points here?
¿Hay aquí corriente eléctrica? [ai akee kor-yenteh elektreeka]

Where can I exchange gas bottles?
¿Dónde puedo cambiar botellas de butano (Am: garrafas de gas)? [dondeh pwedo kamb-yar botayass deh bootano (garafass deh gass)]

advance reservation
previo aviso [preb-yo abeesso]

aluminium foil
el papel de aluminio [el papel deh aloomeenyo]

barbecue/grill lighters
el encendedor [el enthendedor]

barbeque/grill
parrilla [paree-ya], barbacoa [barbako-a]

bottle opener
el abrebotellas [el abrebotayass]

campervan/motorhome
una autocaravana [oona owtokarabana]

campsite
el camping [el kampeeng]

candles
velas [belass]

caravan (trailer)
una caravana (Am: una casa rodante) [oona karabana (oona kassa rodanteh)]

charcoal
el carbón de parrilla [el karbon deh paree-ya]

cooker
hornillo [ornee-yo], horno [orno]

corkscrew
el sacacorchos [el sakakorchoss]

cutlery
los cubiertos [loss koob-yertoss]

detergent/washing powder
el detergente (en polvo) [el deterkhenteh (en polbo)]

dishcloth (dishtowel)
paño para fregar [panyo para fregar]

electric hook-up point
toma de corriente [toma deh kor-yenteh]

electricity
la corriente [la kor-yenteh], la electricidad [la elektreetheedad]

gas bottle	bombona (Am: garrafa) de gas [bombona (garafa) deh gass]
gas cooker	horno de gas [orno deh gass]
hammer, spade	martillo [martee-yo], pala [pala]
hire, hire charge	alquilar [alkeelar], el alquiler [el alkeeler]
laundry pegs	las pinzas de la ropa [lass peenthass deh la ropa]
methylated spirits	el alcohol de quemar [el alko-ol deh kemar]
paper napkins	las servilletas de papel [lass serbee-yetass deh papel]
paraffin, paraffin lamp	petróleo [petrolayo], lámpara de petróleo [lampara deh petrolayo]
plastic bag	bolsa de plástico [bolssa deh plassteeko]
plug (electric)	clavija de enchufe [klabeekha deh enchoofeh]
pocket knife	navaja [nabakha]
rubbish/garbage bags	bolsa de la basura [bolssa deh la bassoora]
service charge/utilisation fee	tasa de utilización [tassa deh ooteelee-thath-yon]
sink	fregadero [fregadero]
sleeping bag	saco de dormir [sako deh dormeer]
socket (electric)	(caja de) el enchufe [(kakha deh) el enchoofeh]
sunshade/parasol	sombrilla [sombree-ya]
tent peg	estaquilla [esstakee-ya]
tin/can opener	el abrelatas [el abrelatass]
torch/flashlight	linterna [leenterna]
washing-up liquid/ dish detergent	el detergente [el deterkhenteh]
(drinking) water	(el) agua (potable) [(el) agwa (potableh)]

AT A YOUTH HOSTEL

Can I hire…?	¿Me pueden alquilar … [meh pweden alkeelar]
…bedding	… ropa de cama? [ropa deh kama]
…a sleeping bag	… un saco de dormir? [oon sako deh dormeer]
The front door is locked at midnight.	La puerta de entrada se cierra a medianoche. [la pwerta deh entrada seh th-yera a med-ya-nocheh]

dormitory	dormitorio [dormeetor-yo]
kitchen	cocina [kotheena]
membership card	la tarjeta de/el carné de socio [la tarkheta deh/el karneh deh soth-yo]
washroom	los lavabos [loss lababoss]
Wi-Fi	el/la wifi [el/la wai-fai]
youth hostel	el albergue juvenil [el albergeh khoobeneel]
youth hostel card	el carné de albergues juveniles [el karneh deh albergess khoobeneeless]

>WHAT DO YOU WANT TO DO?

Whether you want an authentic cooking course, an exciting hiking trip or a great evening of theatre: the next few pages will help you experience loads of holiday adventures.

GENERAL INFORMATION

I'd like a map of..., please.   Quisiera un mapa de …, por favor.
[keessyera oon mapa deh …, por fabor]

What tourist attractions are there here?   ¿Qué cosas dignas de verse hay aquí?
[keh kossass deegnass deh bersseh ai akee]

Are there tours of the city?   ¿Hay visitas organizadas de la ciudad?
[ai beesseetass organeethadass deh la th-yoodad]

How much does the tour cost?   ¿Cuánto cuesta el billete (Am: boleto), por favor?
[kwanto kwessta el bee-yeteh (boleto), por fabor]

A PACKED SCHEDULE

SIGHTSEEING/MUSEUMS

When is the museum open?	¿A qué horas está abierto el museo?
	[a keh orass essta ab-yerto el moossayo]
When does the tour start?	¿A qué hora comienza la visita con guía?
	[a keh ora kom-yentha la beesseeta kon gee-a]
Is there a guided tour in English?	¿Se ofrecen visitas guiadas en inglés?
	[seh ofrethen beesseetass gyadass en eengless]
Is this/that…?	¿Es este/esta/esto …? [ess essteh/essta/essto]

altar	el altar [el altar]
architecture	arquitectura [arkeetektoora]
audio guide	audioguía [owd-yo-gee-a]
building	edificio [edeefeeth-yo]
castle	castillo [kasstee-yo]
cathedral	la catedral [la katedral]
cemetery	cementerio [thementer-yo]
chapel	capilla [kapee-ya]
church	iglesia [eegless-ya]
day trip	la excursión de un día [la eksskoorssyon deh oon dee-a]
emperor, empress	el emperador [el emperador], la emperatriz [la emperatreeth]
excavations	las excavaciones [lass ekss-kabath-yoness]
exhibition	la exposición [la eksssposseeth-yon]
fortress	fortaleza [fortaletha], ciudadela [th-yoodadela]
gallery	galería [galeree-a]
guide	el guía (turístico) [el gee-a (tooreessteeko)]
(guided) tour	visita (guiada) [beesseeta (gee-ada)]
king, queen	el rey [el ray], reina [rayna]
monuments, sights	los monumentos [loss monoomentoss]
museum	museo [moossayo]
painter	el pintor [el peentor], la pintora [la peentora]
painting, picture	pintura [peentoora], cuadro [kwadro]
palace	palacio [palath-yo]
religion	la religión [la releekh-yon]
restore (refurbish)	restaurar [resstowrar]
ruin n	ruina [rweena]
sculptor, sculpture	el escultor [el esskooltor], escultura [esskooltoora]
service (relig.)	servicio [serbeethee-o], oficio [ofeethee-o];
	(mass) misa [meessa]

sightseeing tour of the town/city	visita de la ciudad [beesseeta deh la th-yoodad], las excursiones [lass ekss-koorss-yoness]
square	plaza [platha]
the old town	la ciudad vieja [la th-yoodad bee-ekha]
tower	la torre [la toreh]
town hall, city hall	ayuntamiento [a-yoonta-mee-ento]

TRIPS & TOURS

What time are we meeting?	¿Cuándo quedamos? [kwando kedamoss]
Where are we meeting?	¿De dónde salimos? [deh dondeh saleemoss]
Will we go past the...?	¿Pasamos por ...? [passamoss por]
Are we going to see..., too?	¿Vamos a visitar también ...? [bamoss a beesseetar tam-byen]
When are we coming back?	¿Cuándo regresamos? [kwando regressamoss]

botanical garden	el jardín botánico [el khardeen botaneeko]
countryside	el paisaje [el pa-eess-akheh]
covered market	mercado cubierto [merkado koob-yerto]
day trip	la excursión de un día [la eksskoorssyon deh oon dee-a]
fishing port/harbour	puerto de pescadores [pwerto deh pesskadoress]
fishing village	el lugar de pesca [el loogar deh pesska]
forest	el bosque [el bosskeh]
game/wildlife park	reserva de animales [resserba deh aneemaless]
inland	el interior (del país) [el eenter-yor (del pa-eess)]
island round-trip	visita (guiada) de la isla [beesseeta (gyada) deh la eezla]
lake	lago [lago]
market	mercado [merkado]
mountain village	pueblo de montaña [pweblo deh montanya]
national park	parque m nacional [parkeh nath-yonal]
nature reserve	reserva natural/ecológica [resserba natooral/ekolo-kheeka]
off-road vehicle	todoterreno [todotereno]
peak (mountain)	pico [peeko]
pilgrimage site	el lugar de peregrinación [el loogar deh peregreenath-yon]
plantation	las plantaciones [lass plantath-yoness]
ravine	barranco [baranko]
river	flujo [ftookho], rio [ree-o]
sea	el mar [el mar]
trip	la excursión [la eksskoorssyon]
vantage point	el mirador [el meerador], punto de observación [poonto deh obsserbath-yon]
waterfall	catarata [katarata], cascada [kasskada]
zoo	el zoo [el thoh], el parque zoológico [el parkeh thoh-lokheeko]

AFTER DARK

PUB/BAR/CLUB | PUB/BAR/CLUB [pab/bar/kloob]

What's on...	¿Qué se puede hacer … [keh seh pwedeh ather]
this weekend?	este fin de semana? [essteh feen deh semana]
this evening?	hoy por la tarde/noche? [oy por la tardeh/nocheh]
What is there to do here in the evenings?	¿Qué se puede hacer por aquí por las tardes? [keh seh pwedeh ather por akee por lass tardess]
Is there a nice bar/pub here?	¿Hay por aquí un bar/pub acogedor? [ai por akee oon bar/pab ako-khedor]
Where can we go dancing?	¿Dónde se puede ir aquí a bailar? [dondeh seh pwedeh eer akee a bai-lar]
What kind of music do they play here?	¿Qué tipo de música tocan? [keh teepo deh moosseeka tokan]
A (draught/draft) beer, please.	Una caña/una cerveza (de barril), por favor. [oona kanya/oona therbetha (deh bareel), por fabor]
A glass of red wine, please.	Un vino tinto, por favor. [oon beeno teento, por fabor]
The same again, please.	Otro, por favor. [otro, por fabor]
This round's on me.	Esta ronda la pago yo. [essta ronda la pago yo]
Shall we dance?	¿Bailamos? [bai-lamoss]
band	banda [banda], conjunto [konkhoonto]
bar, club, disco	el bar [el bar], el club (nocturno) [el kloob (noktoornol], discoteca [deesskoteka]
bouncer	portero [portero], portera [portera]
dance v	bailar [bai-lar]
folk music	música de baile [moosseeka deh bai-leh]
gay/lesbian scene	movida gay/para lesbianas [mobeeda gay/para lez-bee-anass]
go out	salir [saleer]
live music	música en directo [moosseeka en deerekto]
party	la fiesta [la fyessta]
pub/bar	el bar/pub [el bar/pab]

THEATRE/CONCERT/CINEMA
TEATRO/CONCIERTO/CINE [tay-atro/konth-yerto/theeneh]

Have you got a diary of events for this week?	¿Tienen ustedes un programa de espectáculos para esta semana? [tyenen oosstedess oon programa deh esspektakooloss para essta semana]
What's on at the theatre tomorrow evening?	¿Qué hay mañana por la tarde en el teatro? [keh ai manyana por la tardeh en el tay-atro]

A PACKED SCHEDULE

Can you recommend a good play?	¿Puede usted recomendarme una buena obra de teatro? [pwedeh oossted rekomendarmeh oona bwena obra deh tay-atro]
When does the performance start?	¿A qué hora comienza la representación? [a keh ora kom-yentha la repressentath-yon]
Where can I get tickets?	¿Dónde se pueden adquirir los billetes (Am: boletos)? [dondeh seh pweden ad-keereer loss bee-yetess (boletoss)]
(Two) tickets for this evening, please.	Dos entradas (Am: boletos) para esta noche, por favor. [doss entradass (boletoss) para essta nocheh, por fabor]
A programme/playbill, please.	¿Me puede dar un programa, por favor? [meh pwedeh dar oon programa, por fabor]
Where's the cloakroom?	¿Dónde está el guardarropa? [dondeh essta el gwardaropa]

audio guide	audioguía [owd-yo-gee-a]
advance booking	venta anticipada [benta anteetheepada]
ballet	el ballet [el bal-et]
box office	caja [kakha]
calendar of events	calendario de actos [kalendar-yo deh aktoss]
cinema	el cine [el theeneh]
concert	concierto [konth-yerto]
film/movie	película [peleekoola], el film [el feelm]
opera	ópera [opera]
performance/screening	espectáculo [esspektakoolo], la sesión [la sess-yon]
play	espectáculo [esspektakoolo], teatro [tay-atro]
premiere	estreno [esstreno]
theatre	teatro [tay-atro]
ticket	entrada [entrada], el billete [el bee-yeteh]

LOCAL KNOWLEDGE

Insider Tip

Sundown to Sunrise

Spanish nightlife starts very late in the evening. Nothing gets going at all in the more stylish bars before 10pm. Discos and clubs only start to fill up after midnight and remain open until well after the sun has made its first appearance of the day. If you still haven't had enough when they finally close their doors, top off the day, top off your morning with hot chocolate and *churros* [chooross] (long, thin Spanish donuts) for breakfast.

see the menu, page 46.

Could you tell me when the... festival takes place, please?	¿Me podría decir cuándo es … el festival de …? [meh podree-a detheer kwando ess … el fessteebal deh]
from... to.../every (2) years	Del … al …/Cada (dos) años. [del … al …/kada (doss) anyoss]
every year in August	Cada año en agosto. [kada anyo en agosto]
Can anyone take part/join in?	¿Puede participar cualquiera? [pwedeh parteetheepar kwal-kyera]

bullfight	la corrida de toros [la koreeda deh toross]
carnival	el carnaval [el karnabal], verbena (San Juan/San Pedro) [berbena (san khwan/san pedro)]
circus	circo [theerko]
festival	el festival [el fessteebal]
fireworks	fuegos artificiales [fwegoss arteefeeth-yaless]
flea market	el mercadillo [ol merkadee-yo]
funfair	feria [fer-ya]
local/village summer festival	fiesta mayor [fyessta ma-yor]
Mardi Gras, Shrove Tuesday	martes de carnaval [martess deh karnabal]
May Day	fiesta del primero de mayo [fyessta del preemero deh ma-yo]
parade, procession	la procesión [la prothessyon], el desfile [el dessfeeleh]
village fête	fiesta local/del pueblo [fyessta lokal/del pweblo]

AT THE BEACH & SPORTS

Is there a strong current?	¿Es fuerte la corriente? [ess fwerteh la kor-yenteh]
Is it dangerous for children?	¿Es peligroso para los niños? [ess peleegrosso para loss neenyoss]
When's low tide/high tide?	¿A qué hora es la marea baja/alta? [a keh ora ess la maraya bakha/alta]

beach	playa [pla-ya]
changing rooms	los vestidores [loss bessteedoress]
current	la corriente [la kor-yenteh]
jellyfish	medusa [medoossa]
kiosk	quiosco [kyossko]
lifeguard	el/la vigilante [el/la beekheelanteh]
nudist beach	playa nudista [pla-ya noodeessta]
sand	arena [arena]
shower	ducha [doocha]
sunshade/parasol	sombrilla [sombree-ya]
swim v	nadar [nadar]

A PACKED SCHEDULE

ACTIVE HOLIDAYS/SPORT
VACACIONES ACTIVAS/DEPORTE [bakath-yoness akteebass/deporteh]

What sports facilities are there here?	¿Qué posibilidades hay aquí de hacer deporte? [keh possee-beelee-dadess ai akee deh ather deporteh]
Is there a... here?	¿Hay por aquí un/una …? [ai por akee oon/oona]
Where can I hire...?	¿Dónde puedo alquilar …? [dondeh pwedo alkeelar]
I'd like to take a... course for beginners/an advanced... course.	Me gustaría hacer un curso de … de principiantes/avanzados. [meh goosstaree-a ather oon koorsso deh … deh preenthee-pyantess/abanthadoss]

contest/match	la competición [la kompeteeth-yon]
defeat n	derrota [derota]
draw/tie n	empatado(s) [empatado(ss)]
lose v, win v	perder [perder], ganar [ganar]
match/game	juego [khwego], partido [parteedo]
race n	carrera [karera]
referee/umpire	árbitro [arbeetro], árbitra [arbeetra]
team/crew	equipo [ekeepo]
victory/win n	victoria [beektor-ya]

WATER SPORTS DEPORTE ACUÁTICO [deporteh akwateeko]

boat hire	el aquiler de barcas [el akeeler deh barkass]
boating licence/permit	el carné náutico [el karneh na-ooteeko]
canoe	canoa [kano-a], piragua [peeragwa]
houseboat	la embarcación habitable [la embarkath-yon abeetableh]
indoor pool	piscina interior [peess-theena eenter-yor]
inflatable/rubber dinghy/boat	bote m neumático [boteh nayoomateeko]
motorboat	(lancha) motora [(lancha) motora]

LOCAL KNOWLEDGE

Insider Tip

▶ Life's a Beach

When lounging on the beach in the south, you'll inevitably come across *vendedores ambulantes* [bendadoress amboolantess] – beach sellers who walk up and down selling drinks, sun lotion, sunglasses, parasols, toys, newspapers... in short, everything you might need for a fun day out at the beach. Spanish beaches also boast *chiringuitos* [cheereengeetoss] – beach bars where you can usually enjoy fish, seafood and cool drinks on the terrace.

open air pool	piscina al aire libre [peess-theena al ai-reh leebreh]
pedalo/pedal boat	barca de pedales [barka deh pedaless]
pick-up service	servicio de recogida [serbeeth-yo deh rekokheeda]
rowing/sailing boat	barca de remos/vela [barka deh remoss/bela]
sailing	la navegación a vela/la excursión en velero
	[la nabegath-yon a bela/la eksskoorssyon en belero]
sailing school	escuela de vela [esskwela deh bela]
surf school	escuela de surf(ing) [esskwela deh soorf[eeng]]
surfboard	tabla deslizadora/de surf [tabla dezleethadora/deh soorf]
surfing	practicar el surf [prakteekar el soorf]
water skiing	el esquí acuático [el esskee akwateeko]
windsurfing	practicar el windsurf [prakteekar el weend-soorf]

DIVING BUCEO [boothayo]

breathing/oxygen apparatus	botella de oxígeno [botaya deh ok-seekheno]
diving equipment	equipo de buceo [ekeepo deh boothayo]
diving mask	las gafas de buceo [lass gafass deh boothayo]
diving school	escuela de buceo [esskwela deh boothayo]
flippers	las aletas (de natación) [lass aletass (deh natath-yon)]
go snorkelling	nadar con tubo de buceo [nadar kon toobo deh boothayo]
wetsuit	el traje isotérmico/de neopreno
	[el trakheh eessotermeeko/deh nayopreno]

FISHING PESCA [pesska]

Where can I go fishing?	¿Dónde se puede pescar a caña?
	[dondeh seh pwedeh pesskar a kanya]

bait	el cebo [el thebo]
deep-sea fishing	pesca marítima/de altura [pesska mareeteema/deh altoora]
fishing licence	licencia de pesca [leethenth-ya deh pesska]
fishing rod	caña de pescar [kanya deh pesskar]
go fishing	pescar con caña [pesskar kon kanya]
off/close season	veda [beda]

BALL GAMES JUEGOS DE PELOTA [khwegoss deh pelota]

ball	pelota [pelota], (larger ball) el balón [el balon]
basketball	baloncesto [balonthessto]
football	el fútbol [el footbol]
football ground	campo (Am: cancha) de fútbol [kampo (kancha) deh footbol]
football team	equipo de fútbol [ekeepo deh footbol]
goal	portería [poreteree-a]
goalkeeper	portero [portero], portera [portera]
net	la red [la red]
volleyball	el balonvolea [el balombolaya]

A PACKED SCHEDULE

TENNIS, ETC. TENIS ETC. [teneess et-thet-era]

badminton	el bádminton [el badmeenton]
table tennis	el ping-pong [el peeng-pong], el tenis de mesa [el teneess deh messa]
tennis, squash	el tenis [el teneess], el squash [el skwash]
tennis court	pista de tenis [peessta deh teneess]
(tennis) racket/racquet	raqueta (de tenis) [[raketa] deh teneess]

FITNESS & WEIGHT TRAINING EJERCICIO FÍSICO Y DE FUERZA [ekhertheeth-yo feesseeko ee deh fwertha]

aerobics, yoga, Pilates	el aerobic [el ai-robeek], el yoga [el yoga], el pilates [el peelatess]
fitness centre	gimnasio [kheem-nass-yo]
fitness training	la preparación física [la preparath-yon feesseeka]
go jogging/jog v	correr [korer]
weight training	ejercicio de fuerza [ekhertheeth-yo deh fwertha]

WELLBEING WELLNESS [wel-ness]

acupressure	la acupresión [la akoopressyon]
aromatherapy	aromaterapia [aromaterapee-a], terapia con aromas [terap-ya kon aromass]
baths/bathhouse	baños [banyoss]
beauty treatment	tratamiento de belleza [trata-mee-ento deh bayetha]
diet foods	alimentos dietéticos [aleementoss dee-et-et-eekoss]
hammam, Turkish bath	baños turcos [banyoss toorkoss]
manicure	manicura [maneekoora]
massage	el masaje [el massakheh]
pedicure	pedicura [pedeekoora]
sauna, steam room	sauna [sowna], baño de vapor [banyo deh bapor]
skin peeling treatment	el peeling [el peeleeng]
solarium	solario [solar-yo]

CYCLING MONTAR EN BICICLETA [montar en beetheekleta]

(electric) bicycle/bike	bicicleta (electrónica) [beetheekleta [elektroneeka]]
crash helmet	casco de bicicleta [kassko deh beetheekleta]
cycle path	pista para bicicletas [peessta para beetheekletass]
cycle race	carrera/vuelta ciclista [karera/bwelta theekleessta]
cycle tour	la excursión en bici(cleta) [la ekss-koor-syon en beethee[kleta]]
cycle v	montar (Am: andar) en bicicleta [montar [andar] en beetheekleta]
(inner) tube	cámara [kamara]
mountain bike	bicicleta de montaña [beetheekleta deh montanya], el mountain bike [el mown-tain baik]
pump	bomba de aire [bomba deh ai-reh]
(puncture) repair kit	los parches y el pegamento [loss parchess ee el pegamento]
racing bike	bicicleta de carreras [beetheekleta deh karerass]

I'd like to go for a hike in the mountains.
Quisiera hacer una excursión por las montañas.
[keessyera ather oona eksskoorssyon por lass montanyass]

Can you show me an interesting route on the map?
¿Puede usted indicarme en el mapa un itinerario interesante? [pwedeh oossted eendeekarmeh en el mapa oon eeteenerar-yo eenteressanteh]

cable car/funicular railway	el funicular [el fooneekoolar], teleférico [telefereeko]
day trip/excursion	la excursión de un día [la ekss-koor-syon deh oon dee-a]
hiking, mountaineering	caminar [kameenar], escalar [esskalar]
hiking map	el mapa [el mapa]
long-distance hiking route	sendero europeo [sendero ayoo-ropayo]
mountain guide	el/la guía de montaña [el/la gee-a deh montanya]
path, route	sendero [sendero], ruta [roota]
safety rope	soga de seguridad [soga deh segooreedad]
St James' Way	Camino de Santiago [kameeno deh sant-yago]

equestrian holidays	las vacaciones a caballo [lass bakath-yoness a kaba-yo]
horse	caballo [kaba-yo]
riding school	escuela de equitación [esskwela deh ekeetath-yon]
ride v/go riding	paseo a caballo [passayo a kaba-yo]

golf course	campo de golf [kampo deh golf]
golf club	raqueta de golf [raketa deh golf]
tee	punto de salida [poonto deh saleeda]
eighteen-hole course	campo de dieciocho hoyos [kampo deh dyeth-yocho oyoss]
visitor	el/la visitante [el/la beesseetanteh]

gliding	volar a vela [bolar a bela]
hang gliding	vuelo libre [bwelo leebreh], ala delta [ala delta]
parachuting	paracaidismo [parakaideezmo]
paragliding	el parapente [el parapenteh]
parasailing	parapendio a motore trainante [parapendee-yo a motoreh traeenanteh]

A day ticket, please.
Un forfait, por favor. [oon forfait, por fabor]

What time is the last trip up the mountain/ down into the valley?
¿A qué hora es la última subida/bajada?
[a keh ora ess la oolteema soobeeda/bakhada]

binding	la fijación (de los esquís)
	[la feekhath-yon (deh loss esskeess)]
cross-country ski course	pista de esquí a fondo [peessta deh esskee a fondo]
cross-country skiing	el esquí de fondo [el esskee deh fondo]
day pass	el forfait (Am: boleto) válido para un día
	[el forfait (boleto) baleedo para oon dee-a]
(ice) hockey	el hockey (sobre hielo) [el ok-ay (sobreh yelo)]
ice rink	pista de hielo [peessta deh yelo]
ice skates	los patines de hielo [loss pateeness deh yelo]
ice skating	el patinaje [el pateenakheh]
ski n, ski v/go skiing	el esquí [el esskee], esquíar [esskee-ar]
ski goggles	las gafas de esquí
	[lass gafass deh esskee]
ski poles	los bastones de esquí
	[loss basstoness deh esskee]
skiing lessons	curso de esquí [koorsso deh esskee]
snowboard n	el snowboard [el znoh-bord]
toboggan	trineo [treenayo]
week pass	abono semanal [abono semanal]

COURSES

I would like to take a Spanish language course...	Me interesa hacer … un curso de español.
	[meh eenteressa ather … oon koorsso deh esspanyol]
...for beginners.	para principiantes [para preentheep-yantess]
...for advanced learners.	de nivel avanzado [deh neebel abanthado]
Is prior knowledge required?	¿Se necesitan conocimientos previos?
	[seh nethesseetan konothee-mee-entoss preb-yoss]
Are materials included in the price?	¿Se incluyen los gastos de material?
	[seh eenklooyen loss gasstoss deh mater-yal]
What should I bring along?	¿Qué se necesita traer? [keh seh nethesseeta tra-er]

carpentry workshop	el taller de carpintería [el ta-yer deh karpeenteree-a]
cooking	cocinar [kotheenar]
flamenco (dancing)	el (baile) flamenco [el (baileh) flamenko]
goldsmithery	labrar orfebrería [labrar orfebrer-ee-a]
life drawing	desnudo [deznoodo]
oil painting	pintura al óleo [peentoora al olayo]
photography	fotografiar [fotograf-yar]
watercolour painting	pintar con acuarela [peentar kon akwarela]
workshop (class)	el taller [el ta-yer]

There's hardly anyone her

(lit: there are four cats here)

Aquí hay cuatro gatos. [akee ai kwatro gato

>WORDS GONE WILD

When your dictionary fails you and everyone seems to be talking gobbledegook, you've most likely been plunged headfirst into the wonderful world of slang.

BECOME **AN INSIDER**

Who hasn't been in this situation: you've made some contacts in a foreign land and are excitedly listening to your new friends chatting away – but their speech is littered with mysterious words that quite simply leave you in the dark. That's because there's a world of difference between the language you'll find in the dictionary and the language people actually use on the street. But don't panic: over the next few pages, we'll plunge you headfirst into the lingo that's spoken in cafés, clubs, bars, shops, hotels and hostels, and show you the way people talk when they're chatting on the bus, on the train, and in the lively

WARNING! SLANG

squares of villages, towns and cities. We've tracked down all the most authentic, essential and downright funniest slang expressions to give you some all-important insider knowledge. But beware: there are some phrases that are better left unsaid! Also, bear in mind that slang is often a very local affair and that pronunciation can vary from region to region. But with a bit of patience, you'll be able to get a handle on all the different regional dialects and listen in on what everyone has to say.

Have fun reading this chapter and broadening your vocabulary!

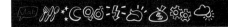

DAY TO DAY

blah

GREETINGS, ETC.

¡Buenas! [bwenass]	Evening!
¡Hola macho! [ola macho]	Hey, man!
¿Qué tal? [keh tal]	How's it going?
¿Qué pasa?/¿Qué va?/¿Qué hay?	What's going on!/What's up!
[keh passa/keh ba/keh ai]	
¡Chao! [chow]/**¡'ta logo!** [ta logo]/**¡Venga!** [benga]	Bye!/Later!/See you later!

RESPONSES

¡Vale! [baleh]	Okay!
¡Legal! [legal]	Exactly!
¡Ajá!/¡Ah! [akha/ah]	Understood!
¡Guau! [goo-ow]	Wow!
¡Caray!/¡Caramba! [karai/karamba]	Damn!
Ni (puta) idea. [nee (poota) eedaya]	Dunno./Not a clue.
Me importa un comino/rábano/pimiento/pepino.	I couldn't care less. (lit: I care a cumin/
[meh eemporta oon komeeno/rabano/peem-yento/pepeeno]	radish/bell pepper/cucumber)
Me la trae floja./Me la suda./Me la pela.	I don't give a shit.
[meh la trai-eh flokha/meh la sooda/meh la pela]	
Paso. [passo]	I can't be arsed/assed.
¡Ni hablar (del peluquín)! [nee ablar (del pelookeen)]	No way!

COMMANDS

¡Marchando!/¡Vamos tirando!	Let's go!
[marchando/bamoss teerando]	
¡Mueve el culo! [mwebeh el koolo]	Move your arse/ass!
¡Ojo! [okho]/**¡Tranqui!** [trankee]	Watch out!
¡Quieto parao! [kyeto parow]	Wait a minute!
¡No te comas el tarro/coco! [no teh komass el taro/koko]	Don't stress out!
¡Ni borracho/a! [nee boracho/a]/**¡Ni loco/a!** [nee loko/a]	Forget it!

AMONG FRIENDS...

pasarse por... [passarsseh por]	to pop in
dar un toque (a alguien) [dar oon tokeh (a alg-yen)]	to ring (s.o.)

WARNING! SLANG

charlar/estar de palique [charlar/esstar deh paleekeh]	to chat
cotillear [kotee-yay-ar]	to gossip
estar de coña [esstar deh konya]	to hang around
decir chorradas [detheer choradass]	to talk bullshit
fardar [fardar]	to boast/brag
un cuento chino [oon kwento cheeno]	a made-up/cock-and-bull story (lit: a Chinese tale)*
meter la pata/la gamba [meter la pata/la gamba]	to put your foot in it/your foot in your mouth
tocar los cojones/huevos/las pelotas a alguien [tokar loss kokhoness/weboss/lass pelotass a alg-yen]	to get on someone's nerves (lit: to feel someone's testicles/eggs/balls)
cabrear (a alguien) [kabray-ar (a alg-yen)]	to piss (s.o.) off/make (s.o.) angry
cabrearse con (alguien) [kabray-arsseh kon (alg-yen)]	to argue with (s.o.)
aguafiestas [agwa-fyesstass]	party-pooper

THAT'S GREAT...

¡(Qué) guay!/¡Qué chulo! [(keh) gwai/keh choolo]	Great!
¡Mola! [mola]	Cool!
¡Esto chuta! [essto choota]	That's fantastic!
cojonudo/la hostia/la leche [kokhonoodo/la osst-ya/la lecheh]	Brilliant!/Great! (leche = lit: milk)
¡Es la leche/monda! [ess la lecheh/monda]	That's amazing!
¡Es lo más! [ess lo mass]	That's the bee's knees!/the bomb!/ the business!
pasarlo pipa/bomba/cañón [passarlo peepa/bomba/kanyon]	to have fun
alucinar/flipar [alootheenar/fleepar]	to flip out/go crazy

THAT'S BORING...

nada del otro jueves [nada del otro khwebess]	nothing to write home about (lit: nothing of last Thursday)
soso [sosso]	boring
ser un rollo/un muermo/un coñazo [ser oon royo/oon mwermo/oon konyatho]	to be boring as hell

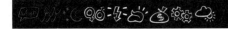

THAT'S ANNOYING

¡Qué chorrada! [keh chorada]	What bullshit!
¡Qué rollo! [keh royo]	What bollocks!
¡Qué gilipollez! [keh kheeleepoyeth]	What baloney!
¡No seas plasta/"pesao" (pesada)!	Don't get on my nerves! (no seas plasta
[no sayss plassta/pessow (pessada)]	= lit: don't be money/moolah)
una patada en los cojones/huevos	a real kick in the nuts
[oona patada en loss kokhoness/weboss]	
una puñetera [oona poonyetera]	a crappy situation

FEELING BAD?

estar pachucho/a [esstar pachoocho/a]	to be under the weather
estar hecho/a polvo [esstar echo/a polbo]	to be exhausted (lit: to be powdered)✱
hacer/echar una cabezadita	to take a nap
[ather/echar oona kabethadeeta]	
meterse en el sobre [metersseh en el sobreh]	to go to bed (lit: to get into the envelope)
quedarse frito/a [kedarsseh freeto/a]	to fall asleep
sobar [sobar]	to sleep
no estar católico/a [no esstar katoleeko/a]	to be unwell (lit: to not be a catholic)
estar chungo/a [esstar choongo/a]	to be ill/sick
estar jodido/a [esstar khodeedo/a]	to be very ill/sick
estar "depre" [esstar depreh]	to be depressed
estar de morros [esstar deh moross]	to sulk
estar "cagao" [esstar kagow]	to be shit-scared
cagarse de miedo [kagarsseh deh mee-edo]	to shit yourself with fear
estar de mala leche/uva [esstar deh mala lecheh/ooba]	to be in a bad mood
	(lit: to be of bad milk/grapes)
estar de un humor de perros	to be in a terrible mood
[esstar deh oon oomor deh peross]	(lit: a dog-mood)
cabrearse [kabray-arsseh]	to flip out/throw a tantrum

WARNING! SLANG

FOOD

papear [papay-ar] — to eat
tapear [tapay-ar] — to go and eat tapas
bocata [bokata] — sandwich
flauta [flowta] — very long sandwich
pincho (de tortilla) [peencho (deh tortee-ya)] — (tortilla) snack
pincho moruno [peencho moroono] — kebab/skewer
chiringuito [cheereengeeto] — snack(bar)
panchitos [pancheetoss] — salty peanuts
champis [champeess] — mushrooms
el bikini [el beekeenee] — (warm) sandwich filled with cheese and cooked ham (lit: the bikini)
el pepito [el pepeeto] — meat sandwich
un montadito/un montao [oon montadeeto/oon montow] — a sandwich with ham or a fillet of pork or beef
comida rápida/comida basura [komeeda rapeeda/komeeda bassoora] — fast food
la gusa [la goossa] — the munchies
Tengo un hambre de mil demonios. [tengo oon ambreh deh meel demonyoss] — I'm starving. (lit: I have a hunger of a thousand demons)
Me muero de hambre. [meh mwero deh ambreh] — I'm dying of hunger.
zampar/devorar [thampar/deborar] — to gobble up/devour
ponerse las botas/ponerse morado [ponersseh lass botass/ponersseh morado] — to stuff yourself with something (ponerse las botas = lit: to put on the boots)
el/la de la vergüenza [el/la deh la bergwentha] — the leftovers
la dolorosa [la dolorossa] — the bill/check (lit: the painful)

GOING OUT

■ DRINKS ■

una copa [oona kopa] — alcoholic drink (lit: a glass)
una caña [oona kanya] — a glass of beer (lit: cane/reed/stalk)
una jarra [oona khara] — a pitcher of beer
un quinto [oon keento] — a small bottle of beer (200 ml)
una mediana [oona med-yana] — a medium bottle of beer (330 ml)
la litrona [la leetrona] — a large bottle of beer (1 litre)
el botellón [el botayon] — a litrona (see above!) that's drunk on the street
una clara [oona klara] — a shandy (mix of lager and lemonade)

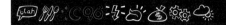

el cubata [el koobata]	a cocktail/long drink
el chato [el chato]	a small glass of wine
mollate [moyateh]	red wine
tinto de verano [teento deh berano]	red wine spritzer with lemonade
un vino peleón [oon beeno pelay-on]	hooch
un sol y sombra [oon sol ee sombra]	a mix of cognac and sweet anise
un carajillo [oon karakhee-yo]	an espresso with brandy

AT THE BAR/PUB

garito/bareto [gareeto/bareto]	bar
antro/cuchitril [antro/koocheetreel]	dive bar/drinking hole
ir de copas [eer deh kopass]	bar crawl
Me muero de sed. [meh mwero deh sed]	I'm dying of thirst.
¡Marchando! [marchando]	Right away!/With you right away!
Me toca (a mí). [meh toka (a mee)]	This is my round.
¡Pa' dentro! [pa dentro]	Down it!/Chug it!
privar/mamar [preebar/mamar]	to drink alcohol
empinar el codo [empeenar el kodo]	to drink alcohol (lit: to raise the elbows)
melopea [melopaya]	a booze-up
echar una cana al aire [echar oona kana al ai-reh]	to paint the town red (lit: to throw a grey hair in the air)
pasar la noche en blanco [passar la nocheh en blanko]	to party all night (lit: to spend the night in white)
el gorila [el goreela]	bouncer (lit: gorilla)
Aquí hay cuatro gatos. [akee ai kwatro gatoss]	There's hardly anyone here. (lit: there are four cats here)
Esto está muerto. [essto essta mwerto]	This place is dead.
estar a tope/de bote en bote [esstar a topeh/deh boteh en boteh]	to be rammed/chock full
menear/mover el esqueleto [menay-ar/mober el esskeleto]	to dance (lit: to move the skeleton)

LATER ON...

estar achispado [esstar acheesspado]	to have had one too many
estar pedo/llevar un pedo [esstar pedo/yebar oon pedo]	to be as drunk as a skunk
estar ciego/a [esstar th-yeh-goo/a]	to be roaring drink (lit: to be blind)*
cogorza/pedo/trompa [kogortha/pedo/trompa]	drunkenness
una resaca [oona ressaka]	a hangover
echar la pota/la papilla [echar la pota/la papee-ya]	to throw up/vomit
estar de bajón [esstar deh bakhon]	to be down in the dumps

WARNING! SLANG

SMOKING

pito/pitillo [peeto/peetee-yo] — cigarette/ciggie/smoke/fag
fumar como un carretero [foomar komo oon karetero] — to smoke like a chimney
(lit: like a cart driver)

MEN & WOMEN

PEOPLE

tipo/tío [teepo/tee-o] — guy/dude (neutral) (tio = lit: uncle)
fulano [foolano] — guy (slightly pejorative)
tía [tee-a] — chick/girl (tia = lit: aunt)
pava [paba] — bitch/cow
estar bueno/a [esstar bweno/a] — to look good
tío bueno/tía buena [tee-o bweno/tee-a bwena] — hot dude/hot chick
maruja [marookha] — a gossip (female)
parienta [par-yenta] — wife
los viejos [loss bee-ekhoss] — the parents (lit: the oldies)
colega/tronco/a [kolega/tronko/a] — pal/mate
basca/peña [basska/penya] — clique

FLIRTING & MORE...

Me hace tilín. [meh atheh teeleen] — I like him/her. (lit: he/she makes me ring)
entrarle (a alguien) [entrarleh (a alg-yen)] — to chat up/hit on s.o.
ligar con... [leegar kon] — to flirt with someone
sobarse [sobarsseh] — to make out
morreo [morayo] — to French kiss
llevarse al huerto (a alguien) — to pick (someone) up
[yebarsseh al werto (a alg-yen)]
tenerla tiesa/dura [tenerla tyessa/doora] — to have an erection

Bar

*

goma/funda/globo [goma/foonda/globo]	rubber/condom
follar/echar un polvo/joder [foyar/echar oon polbo/khoder]	to screw
dar plantón [dar planton]	to dump s.o. (lit: to give a seedling)✳
poner los cuernos [poner loss kwernoss]	to cheat on s.o. (lit: to put the horns on s.o.)
cortar con (alguien) [kortar kon (alg-yen)]	to break up with (s.o.)
Si te he visto, no me acuerdo.	Out of sight, out of mind.
[see teh eh beessto, no meh akwerdo]	
ser un calzonazos [ser oon kalthonathoss]	to be a hen-pecked husband

RANTING, BITCHING, SWEARING

■THE BASICS■

¡Jolín!/¡Jolines!/¡Jope!/¡Jo!	Damn!/Man!
[kholeen/kholeeness/khopeh/kho]	
¡Joder! [khoder]	Fuck!
¡Mierda! [mee-erda]	Shit!
¡Cojones! [kokhoness]	Bollocks!
¡Cierra el pico! [th-yera el peeko]	Shut up!
¡Que te den (morcillas)!/¡Que te zurzan!	Bite me!
[keh teh den (morthee-yass)/keh teh thoorthan]	
¡Métetelo donde te quepa!	You can stick that where the sun
[metetelo dondeh teh kepa]	don't shine!
¡Lárgate!/¡Pírate! [largateh/peerateh]	Go away!
¡Vete a freír espárragos/monas! [beteh a fray-eer	Go screw yourself!
essparagoss/monass]	(espárragos = lit: go and fry asparagus!)
¡Vete a tomar por culo! [beteh a tomar por koolo]	Get lost!
¡Vete a la mierda/al carajo!	Piss off!
[beteh a la mee-erda/al karakho]	(carajo = lit: dick)
tomar el pelo (a alguien) [tomar el pelo (a alg-yen)]	to bust (s.o.'s) balls
poner verde/a parir (a alguien)	to moan/bitch (about s.o.)
[poner berdeh/a pareer (a alg-yen)]	

✳

WARNING! SLANG

■NUMBSKULLS & NITWITS■

"pirao" (pirada) [peerow (peerada)]
weirdo

Es un besugo/un papanatas.
He's/She's a jerk/an idiot.
   [ess oon bessoogo/oon papanatass]

no tener ni (puta) idea de algo
to not have the slightest
   [no tener nee (poota) eedaya deh algo]
   (puta = lit: whore) idea about sth

No entiende ni jota. [no ent-yendeh nee khota]
He/She hasn't got the foggiest.

tonto'l culo [tonto-ol koolo]
as thick as two short planks
   (lit: stupid right down to the arse/ass)

Le falta un tornillo. [leh falta oon tornee-yo]
He/She has a screw loose.

cruzarse los cables (a alguien)
to go crazy (at s.o.)
   [krootharsseh loss kables (a alg-yen)]

"chalao"[chalow]/**chiflado/a** [cheeflado/a]
lunatic

estar como una cabra [esstar komo oona kabra]
to be totally crazy (lit: to be like a goat)

gilipollas [geeleepoyass]
complete idiot

■MORE INSULTS■

un golfo [oon golfo]
crook/wheeler-dealer

guiri [geeree]
tourist

ser hortera [ser ortera]
to have no taste

pijo/a [peekho/a]
trendy, fancy-schmancy type

ser un bocazas [ser oon bokathass]
to have a large trap

petardo/a [petardo/a]
to be all mouth and no brain

sabelotodo [sabelotodo]
smart arse/ass (lit: know-it-all)

chulo/a/chuleta [choolo/a/chooleta]
smug/boaster/blowhard

ser un fantasma [ser oon fantazma]
to be a boaster/a blowhard

empollón (empollona) [empoyon (empoyona)]
nerd/geek/swot

hijo de papá [eekho deh papa]
mummy's boy (lit: daddy's son)

calzonazos [kalthonathoss]
wus/wimp

no tener huevos [no tener weboss]
to be a coward/yellow (lit: to have no eggs)

lamerle el culo (a alguien) [lamerleh el koolo (a alg-yen)] to brown-nose (s.o.)

un lameculos [oon la-me-koo-loss]
an arse licker/ass kisser

ser un jeta/tener morro [ser oon kheta/tener moro]
to be cheeky/barefaced/impertinent

ser un pelma/un pelmazo/un "pesao"
to be a nuisance
   [ser oon pelma/oon pelmatho/oon pessow]

sacar de quicio [sakar deh keeth-yo]
to get on s.o.'s nerves

tener mala leche/uva/sangre
to be in a bad mood
   [tener mala lecheh/ooba/sangreh]
   (lit: to have bad milk/grapes/blood)

un borde [oon bordeh]
a meanie/bitch

¡Cabrón! [kabron]
arse/ass hole! (lit: billy-goat)

¡Hijo de Puta!/¡Joputa! [eekho deh poota/kho-poota]
Son of a bitch! (lit: son of a whore)

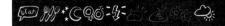

UNMENTIONABLES

mugre [moogreh]	filth/dirt
el tigre [el teegreh]	the bog/can/shitter (lit: tiger)
hacer pipí [ather peepee]	to pee/piss
cambiarle el agua al canario/a las olivas/ a las aceitunas [kamb-yarleh el agwa al kanar-yo/ a lass oleebass/a lass athaytoonass]	to take a leak (lit: to change the canary's water/the olives' water)
mear [may-ar]	to piss
tirarse un "peo" [teerarsseh oon payo]	to fart/let one go
cagar/jiñar [kagar/kheenyar]	to shit
echar la pota [echar la pota]	to vomit

MONEY

■CASH

pelas/pasta/guita/parné [pelass/passta/geeta/parneh]	Moolah/Dosh/Dough
pavos/eurillos/euritos [paboss/ayoo-ree-yoss/ayoo-reetoss]	Euros (pavo = lit: turkey)
calderilla [kalderee-ya]	change

■RICH OR BROKE

un mogollón de pasta [oon mogoyon deh passta]	a chunk of change
estar forrado/a [esstar forado/a]	to be filthy rich
nadar en dinero [nadar en deenero]	to be swimming in money
ganar una pasta gansa [ganar oona passta ganssa]	to be raking it in
un rata/un "agarrao" (agarrada) [oon rata/oon agarow (agarada)]	a miser
estar sin blanca/sin un duro/seco/a [esstar seen blanka/seen oon dooro/sekoo/a]	to be broke
apretarse el cinturón [apretarsseh el theentooron]	to tighten one's belt

WARNING! SLANG

PRICEY OR PEANUTS

¿Cuánto es la broma? [kwanto ess la broma] — What's the damage?

costar un riñón/un ojo de la cara [kosstar oon reenyon/ oon okho deh la kara] — to cost a fortune (lit: to cost a kidney/ an eye from your face)*

carero/a [karero/a] — racketeer/rip-off merchant

clavar [klabar] — to ask too much money for sth

¡Es una clavada! [ess oona klabada] — That's a bit pricey!

un robo/una estafa [oon robo/oona esstafa] — a rip-off/scam

un chollo/una ganga [oon choyo/oona ganga] — a steal/deal

estar "tirao" [esstar teerow] — to be as cheap as chips

SPENDING & EARNING

regatear [regatay-ar] — to bargain

trapicheo [trapeechayo] — a shady deal

timar [teemar] — to rip s.o. off

chorizar/mangar [choreethar/mangar] — to nick/steal

gorrear [goray-ar] — to scrounge/to blag

un gorrón/una gorrona [oon goron/oona gorona] — a freeloader

tirar el dinero por la ventana [teerar el deenero por la bentana] — to throw money out of the window

pulirse el dinero [pooleersseh el deenero] — to drink away one's money

WORK

ponerse las pilas [ponersseh lass peelass] — to get cracking (lit: to put your batteries in)

estar al loro [esstar al loro] — to understand (lit: to be at the parrot)

mileurista [mee-lay-oor-eessta] — a young worker living on €1000/month

currante [kooranteh] — worker

currar [koorar] — to toil/grind away

dar el callo/trabajar como un burro [dar el ka-yo/trabakhar komo oon booro] — to work hard (lit: to work like a donkey)

matarse a trabajar [matarsseh a trabakhar] — to work oneself to death

ser pan comido/ser coser y cantar [ser pan komeedo/ser kosser ee kantar] — to be easy/a snap (lit: to be cooked bread/ to be sewing and singing)

estar "chupao" [esstar choopow] — to be a piece of cake

morirse de asco [moreersseh deh assko] — to bore oneself to death

chapuza [chapootha] — botched job/shoddy work

manazas [manathass] — klutz/blunderer

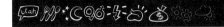

cagarla [kagarla]
to screw sth up

echarle el sermón (a alguien)
[echarleh el sermon (a alg-yen)]
to give (someone) a telling-off/
a bollocking/a tongue-lashing

tener enchufe [tener enchoofeh]
to be well-connected
(lit: to have an electric socket)*

ser un pez gordo [ser oon peth gordo]
to be a big deal

THE WEATHER

¡Menuda rasca! [menooda rasska]
It's so cold!

¡Hace un frío que pela! [atheh oon free-o keh pela]
It's freezing!

¡Hace un frío del carajo!
[atheh oon free-o del karakho]
It's bloody cold!
(lit: it's dick-cold)

quedarse como un témpano
[kedarsseh komo oon tempano]
to be stiff with cold
(lit: to be like an ice floe)

Está lloviendo a cántaros.
[essta yob-yendo a kantaross]
It's raining buckets.
(lit: it's raining jars)

estar empapado/a [esstar empapado/a]
to be soaking wet

estar calado/a hasta los huesos
[esstar kalado/a assta loss wessoss]
to be soaked through

el lorenzo [el lorentho]
the sun

un calor infernal/calor sofocante
[oon kalor eemfernal/kalor sofokanteh]
scorching heat

el bochorno [el bochorno]
muggy/close weather

estar (rojo/a) como una gamba
[esstar (rokho/a) komo oona gamba]
to be (as red as) a lobster
(lit: as a prawn)

darse un remojón [darsseh oon remokhon]
to go into the water

¡El agua está buena! [el agwa essta bwena]
The water's lovely!

*

CREDITS

Cover photograph: mauritius images: imagebroker
Photos: Denis Pernath (pp. 2, 3, 6/7, 10/11, 20/21, 54/55, 78/79, 104/105);
Guenter Standl/laif (pp. 3, 36/37); Cortina Hotel, München (pp. 68/69)
Illustrations: Mascha Greune, Munich
'Point & Show' Pictures/Photos: Lazi&Lazi; Food Collection; Comstock;
stockbyte; Fisch-Informationszentrum e.V.; Fotolia/Christian Jung;
Fotolia/ExQuisine; photos.com
Picture editors: Factor Product, Munich (pp. 2, 3, 6/7, 10/11, 20/21, 36/37,
54/55, 68/69, 78/79, 104/105); red.sign, Stuttgart (pp. 41–45)
'Point & Show' Pictures/Illustrations: Factor Product, Munich; HGV Hanseatische
Gesellschaft für Verlagsservice, München (pp. 44/45, 56, 58/59, 62, 66, 73, 75)

1st Edition 2014
Worldwide Distribution: Marco Polo Travel Publishing Ltd, Pinewood, Chineham
Business Park, Crockford Lane, Basingstoke, Hampshire RG24 8AL, United
Kingdom. E-mail: sales@marcopolouk.com
© MAIRDUMONT GmbH & Co. KG, Ostfildern
© based on the PONS Spanish Travel Phrasebook
© PONS GmbH, Stuttgart

Chief editor: Marion Zorn, MAIRDUMONT
Concept and project management: Carolin Schmid, C.C.SCHMID Munich

Edited by: Sonia Aliaga López, Wiesloch;
M. Carmen Almendros de la Rosa, Hamburg
Editing: PONS GmbH, Stuttgart; Kristin Schimpf, MAIRDUMONT, Ostfildern;
Barbara Pflüger, Stuttgart

"Warning! Slang" Chapter:
Editing: MAIRDUMONT, Ostfildern; Bintang Buchservice GmbH, Berlin
Author: Carlos Ródenas Vidiella; Carlos Romero-Garcia, Berlin

Translated from German by J. Andrews, jonandrews.co.uk
Phonetics by J. Andrews, jonandrews.co.uk
Typesetting & Prepress: M. Feuerstein, Wigel

Coverdesign: Factor Product, Munich
Design content: Zum goldenen Hirschen, Hamburg; red.sign, Stuttgart

Printed in Germany

MIX
Paper from
responsible sources
FSC® C004599

> READY FOR ANYTHING

At the Doctor's, at the police station or at the bank: when things get tricky or need to be sorted out fast, this handy chapter will help you out.

BANK/BUREAU DE CHANGE

 Numbers: Inside front cover

Where's the nearest bank, please?	Por favor, ¿dónde hay por aquí un banco? [por fabor, dondeh ai por akee oon banko]
I'd like to change... pounds (dollars) into euros/pesos.	Quisiera cambiar … libra esterlina (dólar m) en euro/peso. [keessyera kamb-yar... leebra essterleena (dolar) en ayooro/pesso]

FROM A TO Z

I'd like to change this traveller's cheque/check.	Quisiera cobrar este cheque de viaje. [keessyera kobrar essteh chekeh deh bee-akheh]
May I see your...	¿Puedo ver ... [pwedo ber]
passport, please?	su pasaporte, por favor? [soo passaporteh, por fabor]
identity card, please?	su carné de identidad, por favor? [soo karneh deh eedenteedad, por fabor]
Sign here, please.	¿Quiere firmar aquí, por favor? [kyereh feermar akee, por fabor]
The cashpoint won't accept my card.	El cajero automático no acepta mi tarjeta. [el kakhero owtomateeko no athepta mee tarkheta]
The cashpoint has swallowed my card.	El cajero automático no me devuelve la tarjeta. [el kakhero owtomateeko no meh debwelbeh la tarkheta]

amount	el importe [el eemporteh], suma [sooma]
bank	banco [banko]
banknote	el billete (de banco) [el bee-yeteh (deh banko)]
bureau de change	oficina/casa de cambio [ofeetheena/kassa deh kamb-yo]
cash register	caja [kakha]
cashpoint	cajero automático [kakhero owtomateeko]
change	(las) monedas [(lass) monedass], dinero suelto [deenero swelto]
change (money) v	cambiar [kamb-yar]
(traveller's) cheque/check	el cheque (de viaje) [el chekeh (deh bee-akheh)]
coin, currency	moneda [moneda]
counter	la ventanilla (Am: boletería) [la bentanee-ya (boleteree-a)]
credit card	tarjeta de crédito [tarkheta deh kredeeto]
exchange (rate)	(tipo de) cambio [(teepo deh) kamb-yo]
form	impreso [eempresso], formulario [formoolar-yo]
money	dinero [deenero]
pay out v	pagar [pagar]
pin number/code	número secreto [noomero sekreto], la clave [la klabeh]
signature	firma [feerma]

COLOURS

Point & Show: page 4

beige	beige [baysh]
black, /white	negro [negro], blanco [blanko]
blue	azul [athool]
brown	marrón [maron]
colourful	de colores [deh koloress], multicolor [moolteekolor]
dark blue, dark green	azul oscuro [athool osskooro], verde oscuro [berdeh osskooro]
golden, silver	dorado [dorado], plateado [pla-tay-ado]
green	verde [berdeh]
grey	gris [greess]
light blue, light green	azul claro [athool klaro], verde claro [berdeh klaro]
orange	naranja [narankha]
pink	rosa [rossa]
plain/monochrome	de un solo color [deh oon solo kolor]
purple	lila [leela], malva [malba]
red	rojo [rokho]
turquoise	turquesa [toorkessa]
violet	violeta [bee-oleta]
yellow	amarillo [amaree-yo]

AT THE DOCTOR'S

■ INFORMATION | LA INFORMACIÓN [la eemformath-yon]

Can you recommend a good...	¿Puede usted indicarme un buen … [pwedeh oossted eendeekarmeh oon bwen]
doctor?; dentist?	médico? [medeeko]; dentista? [denteessta]
eye specialist?; ear, nose and throat specialist?	oculista? [okooleessta]; otorrinolaringólogo? [oto-reeno-lareen-gol-golo]
gynaecologist?; urologist?	ginecólogo? [kheenekologo]; urólogo [oorologo]
dermatologist?	dermatólogo? [dermatologo]
pediatrician?	puericultor? [pweree-kooltor]; pediatra? [ped-yatra]
Where's his/her surgery/ office?	¿Dónde está la consulta (Am: el consultorio)? [dondeh essta la konssoolta (el konssooltor-yo)]

 Pharmacy: page 57, 58, 60

■ AT THE DOCTOR'S | EN LA CONSULTA DEL MÉDICO [en la konssoolta del medeeko]

What's the problem?	¿Qué molestias si ente? [keh molesst-yass see enteh]
It hurts here.	Me duele aquí. [meh dweleh akee]
I've hurt myself.	Me he hecho una herida. [meh eh echo oona ereeda]
I've got a headache.	Tengo dolor de cabeza. [tengo dolor deh kabetha]
I've got a sore throat.	Tengo dolor de garganta. [tengo dolor deh garganta]
I've got a cough.	Tengo tos. [tengo toss]
I'm allergic to...	Soy alérgico/a a … [soy alerkheeko/a a]
antibiotics.	los antibióticos. [loss anteebee-oteekoss]
bees.	las abejas. [lass abekhass]
pollen.	al polen. [al polen]
I'm vaccinated against...	Estoy vacunado/a contra … [esstoy bakoonado/a kontra]
hepatitis A/B/A and B.	la hepatitis A/B/A y B. [la epateeteess ah/beh/ah ee beh]
tetanus./typhoid.	el tétano. [el tetano], el tifus. [el teefooss]
How often do I have to take it?	¿Cuántas veces al día tengo que tomármelo/a? [kwantass bethss al dee-a tengo keh tomarmelo/a]
I'm pregnant.	Estoy embarazada. [esstoy embarathada]
I suffer from...	Soy … [soy]
diabetes./epilepsy.	diabético/a. [dyabeteeko/a]/ epiléptico/a. [epeelepteeko/a]
Where does it hurt?	¿Dónde le duele? [dondeh leh dweleh]
It's nothing serious.	No es nada grave. [no ess nada grabeh]
Can you give me something for...?	¿Podría usted darme algo contra …? [podree-a oossted darmeh algo kontra]
I usually take...	Normalmente tomo … [normalmenteh tomo]

AT THE DENTIST'S
EN LA CONSULTA DEL DENTISTA [en la konssoolta del denteessta]

I've got (terrible) toothache.	Tengo (mucho) dolor de muelas.
	[tengo (moocho) dolor deh mwelass]
This tooth (on the top row/ on the bottom row/in the front of my mouth/in the back of my mouth) hurts.	Me duele este diente (arriba/abajo/delante/atrás).
	[meh dweleh essteh dyenteh (areeba/abakho/delanteh/atrass)]
I've lost a filling.	Se me ha perdido un empaste (Am: una tapadura).
	[seh meh a perdeedo oon empassteh (oona tapadoora)]
I will have to fill the tooth.	Tengo que empastárselo. [tengo keh empasstarsselo]
I will have to pull out the tooth.	Tengo que sacárselo. [tengo keh sakarsselo]
I'd like an injection, please.	Póngame una inyección, por favor.
	[pongameh oona eenyek-thyon, por fabor]
I don't want an injection.	No me ponga una inyección, por favor.
	[no meh ponga oona eenyek-thyon, por fabor]

IN HOSPITAL | EN EL HOSPITAL [en el osspeetal]

How long will I have to stay here?	¿Cuánto tiempo tendré que quedarme aquí?
	[kwanto tyempo tendreh keh kedarmeh akee]
When can I get out of bed?	¿Cuándo podré levantarme? [kwando podreh lebantarmeh]

abdomen	el abdomen [el abdomen]
abscess	absceso [abss-thesso]
AIDS	el sida [el seeda]
allergy	alergia [alerkhee-a]
anaesthetic	anestesia [anesstessya]
ankle	tobillo [tobee-yo]
appendix	el apéndice [el apendeetheh]
arm	brazo [bratho]
artificial limb	la prótesis [la protesseess]
asthma	el asma [el azma]
back	espalda [esspalda]
backache	los dolores de espalda [loss doloress deh esspalda]
bandage	los vendajes [loss bendakhess]
belly	el vientre [el bee-entreh]
blackout	desmayo [dezma-yo]
bladder	vejiga [bekheega]
blood, bleed v	la sangre [la sangreh], sangrar [sangrar]
blood poisoning	la intoxicación de la sangre [la eentoksseekath-yon deh la sangreh]
blood pressure	la tensión (arterial) [la tenssyon [arter-yal]]

bone	hueso [wesso]
brain	cerebro [therebro]
brain hemorrhage	apoplejía [apoplekhee-a], hemorragia cerebral [emorakh-ya therebral]
breathe v	respirar [resspeerar]
broken	roto [roto]
bronchitis	la bronquitis [la bronkeeteess]
bruise	la contusión [la kontoossyon]
bruising	la contusión [la kontoossyon], magulladura [magoo-yadoora]
burn n	quemadura [kemadoora]
bypass	el bypass [el bai-pass]
cancer	el cáncer [el kanther]
catch a cold	resfriarse [ress-free-arsseh]
chest	pecho [pecho]
chickenpox	varicela [bareethela]
chills/shivering	escalofríos [esskalofree-oss]
circulatory disorder	los trastornos de la circulación [loss trasstornoss deh la theerkoolath-yon]
cold	constipado (Am: resfrío) [konssteepado (ress-free-o)]
colic	cólico [koleeko]
collarbone	clavícula [klabeekoola]
concussion	la conmoción cerebral [la kommoth-yon therebral]
constipation	estreñimiento [esstrenyee-mee-ento]
contagious	contagioso [kontakh-yosso]
cough	la tos [la toss]
cramp	el calambre [el kalambreh], espasmo [esspazmo]
cut n	la herida [la ereeda], el corte [el korteh]
diabetes	la diabetes [la dyabetess]

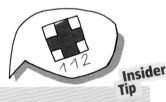

LOCAL KNOWLEDGE

Insider Tip

First Aid

There are three main places to go for help when you're having health problems in Spain. You can either head to a local, state-run *ambulatorio* [amboolator-yo] ("walk in clinic"), a private *centro médico* [chentro medeeko] ("medical centre") or to the nearest *urgencias* [oorgentheeass], the emergency department of a state-run hospital. Brace yourself for long waiting times when you visit any of the state establishments. If you need an ambulance (*ambulancia* [amboolanthee-a]), either call the local emergency services or dial 112, the national emergency number for the police, fire and ambulance services.

diarrhoea	diarrea [dee-ar-aya]
difficulty breathing	las dificultades de respiración
	[lass deefeekooltadess deh resspeerath-yon]
digestion	la digestión [la deekhesst-yon]
dizziness	mareo [marayo], vértigo [berteego]
dress v (a wound)	vendar [bendar]
ear	oreja [orekha]
eardrum	tímpano [teempano]
examination	el examen [el ekssamen]
extract v	sacar [sakar]
eye	ojo [okho]
face	cara [kara]
faint n	desmayo [dezma-yo]
fever	la fiebre [la fyebreh]
filling	el empaste (Am: la tapadura) [el empassteh (la tapadoora)]
finger	dedo [dedo]
flu	la gripe [la greepeh]
food poisoning	la intoxicación [la eentoksseekath-yon]
foot	el pie [el pee-yeh]
fracture	fractura [fraktoora]
fungal infection	la micosis [la meekosseess], los hongos [loss ongoss]
gall bladder	la vesícula [la besseekoola]
German measles	rubeola [roobay-ola]
gullet	esófago [essofago]
hand	la mano [la mano]
head	cabeza [kabetha]
headache	el dolor de cabeza [el dolor deh kabetha]
heart	el corazón [el korathon]
heart attack	el ataque cardíaco [el atakeh kardee-ako],
	infarto cardíaco [eemfarto kardee-ako]
heart trouble	los trastornos cardíacos [loss trasstornoss kardee-akoss]
hernia	hernia [ern-eea]
herpes	el herpes [el erpess]
hip	cadera [kadera]
HIV positive	seropositivo [sero-posseeteebo]
hospital	el hospital [el osspeetal]
hurt v	doler [doler]
ill/sick adj	enfermo [emfermo]
illness	la enfermedad [la emfermedad]
indigestion	la indigestión [la eendeekhesst-yon]
infection	la infección [la eemfek-thyon]
inflammation	la inflamación [la eemflamath-yon]
inflammation of the (middle) ear	la otitis media [la oteeteess med-ya]

injection	la inyección [la eenyek-thyon]
injury	herida [ereeda]
insomnia	insomnio [eenssom-nyo]
intestines	intestino [eentessteeno]
jaundice	ictericia [eektereeth-ya]
joint	la articulación [la arteekoolath-yon]
kidney stone	cálculo renal [kalkoolo renal]
knee	rodilla [rodee-ya]
leg	pierna [pyerna]
lip	el labio [el lab-yo]
liver	hígado [eegado]
lower back pain	lumbago [loombago]
lung	el pulmón [el poolmon]
Lyme disease	la borreliosis [la borel-yo-seess]
measles	el sarampión [el saramp-yon]
medical insurance card	el volante del seguro [el bolanteh del segooro]
meningitis	la meningitis [la meneen-kheeteess]
menstruation	la menstruación [la mensstroo-ath-yon], el período [el peree-odo]
migraine	jaqueca [khakeka]
miscarriage	aborto (involuntario) [aborto (eemboloontar-yo)]
mouth	boca [boka]
mumps	las paperas [lass paperass]
muscle	músculo [moosskoolo]
nausea	las náuseas [lass nowssayass]
neck	cuello [kwayo]
nephritis	la nefritis [la nefreeteess]
(kidney inflammation)	
nerve	nervio [nerb-yo]
nervous	nervioso [nerb-yosso]
nose	la nariz [la nareeth]
nurse	enfermera [emfermera]
operation	la operación [la operath-yon]
pacemaker	el marcapasos [el markapassoss]
pain	los dolores [loss doloress]
paralysis	la parálisis [la paraleesseess]
poisoning	el envenenamiento [el embenena-mee-ento], la intoxicación [la eentoksseekath-yon]
polio	la polio(mielitis) [la pol-yo-(mee-eleeteess)]
pregnancy	embarazo [embaratho]
pregnant	embarazada [embarathada]
prescribe	recetar [rethetar], prescribir [presskreebeer]
pull/strain (a muscle)	la distensión [la deesstenssyon]
pulse	pulso [poolsso]
rash	la erupción cutánea [la eroopth-yon kootanaya]

reception	la recepción [la rethepth-yon]
rheumatism	el reúma [el ray-ooma]
rib	costilla [kosstee-ya]
salmonella	las salmonelas [lass salmonelass]
scar	la cicatriz [la theekatreeth]
scarlet fever	escarlatina [esskarlateena]
sciatica	ciática [th-yateeka]
sexual organs	los órganos genitales [loss organoss kheneetaless]
shin	tibia [teeb-ya], espinilla [esspeenee-ya]
shoulder	hombro [ombro]
sinusitis	la sinusitis [la seenoo-seeteess]
skin	la piel [la pyel]
skull	cráneo [kranayo]
sleeplessness	insomnio [eenssom-nyo]
smallpox	viruela [beeroo-ela]
sore throat	el dolor de garganta [el dolor deh garganta]
specialist	el/la especialista [el/la esspeth-ya-leessta]
sprained	dislocado [deezlokado]
sting	picadura [peekadoora], pinchazo [peenchatho]
stomach	estómago [esstomago]
stomachache	el dolor de estómago [el dolor deh esstomago]
stools	la deposición [la deposseeth-yon]
stroke	el ataque de apoplejía [el atakeh deh apople-khee-a]
sunstroke	la insolación [la eenssolath-yon]
surgery	consulta [konssoolta]
sweat v	sudar [soodar]
swelling	la hinchazón [la eenchathon]
swollen	hinchado [eenchado]
temperature (fever)	la fiebre [la fyebreh]
tetanus	tétano [tetano]
throat	garganta [garganta]
tick	garrapata [garapata]
toe	el dedo del pie [el dedo del pyeh]
tongue	lengua [lengwa]
tonsils	las amígdalas [lass ameegdalass]
tooth	el diente [el dyenteh]
tooth decay	agujero (en el diente) [agookhero (en el dyenteh)]
torn ligament	rotura de ligamentos [rotoora deh leegamentoss]
typhoid	el tifus [el teefooss]
ulcer	úlcera [oolthera]
ultrasonic scan	reconocimiento con ultrasonido [rekonothee-mee-ento kon ooltra-soneedo]
unconscious	desmayado [dezma-yado], desvanecido [dessbanetheedo]
urine	orina [oreena]

vaccination	vacuna [bakoona]
venereal disease	la enfermedad venérea [la emfermedad beneraya]
virus	el virus [el beerooss]
vomit v	vomitar [bomeetar], devolver [debolber]
waiting room	sala de espera [sala deh esspera]
wind n	flato [flato]
wound	herida [ereeda]
x-ray n	una radiografía [oona rad-yo-grafee-a]

INTERNET CAFÉS

Is there an Internet café near here?	¿Dónde hay por aquí un cibercafé? [dondeh ai por akee oon theeberkafeh]
What does it cost for an hour/a quarter of an hour?	¿Cuánto cobran por una hora/un cuarto de hora? [kwanto kobran por oona ora/oon kwarto deh ora]
Can I skype here?	¿Puedo conectarme aquí a skype? [pwedo konektarmeh akee a skaip]
Can I charge my device here?	¿Podría recargar aquí mi dispositivo (electrónico)? [podree-a rekargar akee mee deessposseeteebo (elektroneeko)]
Do you have the right kind of charger for my device?	¿Tiene un recargador/cable de recarga para este tipo de dispositivo? [tyeneh oon rekargador/kableh deh rekarga para essteh teepo deh deessposseeteebo]
Can I print out a page?	¿Puedo imprimir una página? [pwedo eempreemeer oona pakheena]
Can I burn photos from my digital camera onto CD here?	¿Puedo pasar mis fotos de la cámara a un CD? [pwedo passar meess fotoss deh la kamara a oon theh-deh]
Do you have a headset for making phone calls?	¿Tiene (usted) unos cascos para hablar por teléfono? [tyeneh (oossted) oonoss kasskoss para ablar por telefono]

LOST & FOUND

Where's the lost property office, please?	Por favor, ¿dónde está la oficina de objetos perdidos? [por fabor, dondeh essta la ofeetheena deh obkhetoss perdeedoss]
I've lost...	He perdido ... [eh perdeedo]
I left my handbag on the train.	He olvidado mi bolso en el tren. [eh olbeedado mee bolsso en el tren]
Please let me know if it's handed in.	¿Sería tan amable de avisarme si lo encuentran? [seree-a tan amableh deh abeessarmeh see lo enkwentran]
Here's the address of my hotel.	Aquí tiene la dirección de mi hotel. [akee tyeneh la deerek-thyon deh mee otel]

MAIL

Where's... ¿Dónde está … [dondeh essta]

the nearest post office la oficina de correos más cercana?
[la ofeetheena deh korayoss mass therkana]

the nearest postbox el buzón más cercano?
(mailbox)? [el boothon mass therkano]

How much does it cost to ¿Cuánto cuesta una carta/una postal para …
send a letter/a postcard... [kwanto kwessta oona karta/oona posstal para]

to the UK?/to the US?/ el Reino Unido? [el rayno ooneedo]/los Estados Unidos?
to Canada?/to Ireland [loss esstadoss ooneedoss]/Canadá? [kanada]/Irlanda? [eeirlanda]

I'd like to send this letter by Quisiera enviar esta carta por correo aéreo/urgente.
airmail/express. [keessyera emb-yar essta karta por korayo a-erayo/oorkhenteh]

address, addressee la dirección [la deerek-thyon], destinatario [dessteenatar-yo]
by airmail por correo aéreo [por korayo a-erayo]
charge n tarifa [tareefa]
counter la ventanilla (Am: boletería) [la bentanee-ya (boleteree-a)]
envelope, letter, postcard el sobre [el sobreh], carta [karta], la postal [la posstal]
express letter carta urgente [karta oorkhenteh], expreso [eksspresso]
parcel el paquete [el paketeh]
post code código postal [kodeego posstal]
post office oficina de correos [ofeetheena deh korayoss]
postage franqueo [frankayo]
postbox/mailbox el buzón [el boothon]
sender el/la remitente [el/la remeetenteh]
stamp n sello (Am: estampilla) [sayo (esstampee-ya)]
fill in rellenar [rayenar]
post/mail v enviar [emb-yar], expedir [eksspedeer]
stamp v franquear [frankay-ar]
weight peso [pesso]

ON THE PHONE

I'd like... Quiero … [kyero]
a phone card. una tarjeta telefónica. [oona tarkheta telefoneeka]
to reverse the charges. hacer una llamada a cobro revertido.
[ather oona yamada a kobro reberteedo]

an international telephone una tarjeta telefónica de prepago internacional,
card, please. por favor. [oona tarkheta telefoneeka deh prepago eenternath-yonal,
por fabor]

What's the national/ area code for...?	¿Cuál es el prefijo de …? [kwal ess el prefeekho deh]
I'd like to phone...	Quiero que me comuniquen con … [kyero keh meh komooneeken kon]
How much does it cost per minute?	¿Cuánto cuesta cada minuto? [kwanto kwessta kada meenooto]
This is... speaking.	Soy … [soy]; (the person receiving the call usually answers): ¿Diga? [deega]

answer the phone	descolgar [desskolgar]
(phone) call n	llamada telefónica [yamada telefoneeka]
call v	llamar por teléfono [yamar por telefono], telefonear telefonay-ar]
charge	tarifa [tareefa]
charger	el recargador [el rekargador], cable de recarga [kableh deh rekarga]
dial v	marcar (el número) [markar (el noomero)]
directory enquiries	Información f [eemformath-yon]
engaged	ocupado [okoopado], comunicando [komooneekando]
international call	llamada internacional [yamada eenternath-yonal]
local call	llamada interurbana [yamada eenteroorbana]
long-distance call	llamada de larga distancia [yamada deh larga deesstanth-ya]
make a phone call	telefonear [telefonay-ar]
mobile phone	teléfono móvil (Am: cedular) [telefono mobeel (sedoolar)], el móvil [el mobeel]
national/area code	prefijo [prefeekho]
phone call/conversation	llamada [yamada]
phone card	tarjeta telefónica [tarkheta telefoneeka]

LOCAL KNOWLEDGE

Insider Tip

¿Diga?

When you call a Spanish speaker on the phone, you'll be greeted with one of a number of concise phrases. These include: *¿Bueno?* [bweno] (lit: "good"), *¿Aló?* [aloh] (a form of "hello" only used on the phone), *¿Sí?* [see] ("yes") and *¿Diga?/¿Dígame?* [deega/deegameh] (lit: „speak"/"speak to me"). All of them are short, sweet, and get straight to the point, allowing you to get on with your conversation.

phone number	número de teléfono [noomero deh telefono]
prepaid card	tarjeta prepago [tarkheta prepago]
reverse-charge/collect call	llamada a cobro revertido [yamada a kobro reberteedo]
SIM card	tarjeta SIM [tarkheta seem]
smartphone	el smartphone [el zmart-fon]
telephone	teléfono [telefono]
telephone directory	guía telefónica [gee-a telefoneeka]

■ MOBILE PHONE | (TELÉFONO) MÓVIL [(telefono) mobeel]

There's nothing left on my prepaid card.	Mi tarjeta (prepago) no tiene saldo./ Me he quedado sin saldo en la tarjeta. [mee tarkheta (prepago) no tyeneh saldo/meh eh kedado seen saldo en la tarkheta]
I'd like to top up my card.	Quiero recargar mi tarjeta. [kyero rekargar mee tarkheta]
How much call time do I get with a card for (amount of money)?	¿Cuánto tiempo puedo telefonear con la tarjeta de … euros? [kwanto tyempo pwedo telefonay-ar kon la tarkheta deh … ayoo-ross]
What region is this SIM card valid for?	¿Cuál es el área de cobertura de esta tarjeta SIM? [kwal ess el araya deh kobertoora deh essta tarkheta seem]
Please give me a price list/ the tarif information.	¿Me podría dar un informe de las tarifas? [meh podree-a dar oon eemformeh deh lass tareefass]
Have you got prepaid cards for (network provider)?	¿Venden tarjetas de prepago de …? [benden tarkhetass deh prepago deh]
My battery's empty. Do you have a charger I could use?	Me he quedado sin batería. ¿Tienen un recargador/ cable de recarga? [meh eh kedado seem bateree-a tyenen oon rekargador/kableh deh rekarga]

TAKING PHOTOS

 Point & Show: page 59

Do you mind if I take a picture of you?	¿Puedo sacarle una foto? [pwedo sakarleh oona foto]
Am I allowed to take pictures here?	¿Se pueden hacer fotos? [seh pweden ather fotoss]
Would you mind taking a photo of us?	¿Sería tan amable de hacernos una fotografía? [seree-a tan amableh deh athernoss oona fotografee-a]
Just press this button.	Pulse este botón, por favor. [poolsseh essteh boton, por fabor]
That's very kind.	Es muy amable. [ess mwee amableh]

POLICE

Where's the nearest police station, please?	Por favor, ¿dónde está la comisaría de policía más cercana? [por fabor, dondeh essta la komeessaree-a deh poleethee-a mass therkana]
I'd like to report... a theft./an accident.	Quiero denunciar ... [kyero denoonth-yar] un robo. [oon robo]/un accidente. [oon aktheedenteh]
I've been mugged/raped.	Me han asaltado/violado. [meh an assaltado/bee-olado]
My... handbag/wallet/ camera/car has been stolen.	Me han robado ... el bolso/el monedero/mi cámara fotográfica/mi coche. [meh an robado ... el bolsso/el monedero/ mee kamara fotografeeka/mee kocheh]
My car has been broken into.	Me han forzado la puerta del coche. [meh an forthado la pwerta del kocheh]
I've lost...	He perdido ... [eh perdeedo]
My son/daughter is missing.	Ha desaparecido mi hijo/mi hija. [a dessaparetheedo mee eekho/mee eekha]
Can you help me, please?	¿Puede usted ayudarme, por favor? [pwedeh oossted a-yoodarmeh, por fabor]
I'd like to speak to a lawyer.	Quiero hablar con un abogado. [kyero ablar kon oon abogado]

arrest v	arrestar [aresstar]
attack	la agresión [la agressyon]
bank card	tarjeta bancaria/del banco [tarkheta bankar-ya/del banko]
beat up v	golpear [golpay-ar], pegar [pegar]
break into/open	forzar [forthar], violentar [bee-olentar]

LOCAL KNOWLEDGE

Insider Tip

¿To Protect and Serve?

The Spanish police is divided up into a confusing array of forces, making it difficult to know exactly who's responsible for what. The local police (*Policía Local* [poleethee-a local] or *Policía Municipal* [poleethee-a mooneetheepal]), who wear blue and black uniforms with a black and white chequered pattern, deal with thefts and break-ins, settle disputes between neighbours and altercations in bars, and are responsible for controlling the traffic in towns and cities. The blue-clad *Policía Nacional* [poleethee-a nathee-onal] ("national police") sort out personal injuries and property damage and are responsible for issues with personal documents. Finally, the *Guardia Civil* [gardee-a theeveel], dressed in green, control the borders and are responsible for the traffic on country roads.

car radio	la autoradio [la owtorad-yo], la radio del coche [la rad-yo del kocheh]
car key	las llaves del coche [lass yabess del kocheh]
cheque/check	el cheque [el chekeh]
confiscate	confiscar [komfeesskar]
court	el tribunal [el treeboonal]
crime	el crimen [el kreemen]
drugs	las drogas [lass drogass]
harass	molestar [molesstar], importunar [eemportoonar]
identity card	el carné de identidad [el karneh deh eedenteedad]
judge	el juez [el khweth], la juez(a) [la khweth(a)]
key	la llave [la yabeh]
lawyer	abogado [abogado], abogada [abogada]
lose	perder [perder]
money	dinero [deenero]
papers, documents	los documentos [loss dokoomentoss]
passport	el pasaporte [el passaporteh]
pickpocket	ratero/ratera [ratero, ratera], el ladrón/la ladrona [el ladron, la ladrona]
police	policía [poleethee-a]
policeman/policewoman	el/la policía [el/la poleethee-a]
prison	la cárcel [la karthel]
purse, wallet	monedero [monedero], cartera [kartera]
rape	la violación [la bee-olath-yon]
report v	denunciar [denoonth-yar]
theft	robo [robo]
thief	el ladrón [el ladron]

TOILETS & BATHROOMS

Where is the toilet, please?	¿Dónde está el baño, por favor? [dondeh essta el banyo, por fabor]
May I use your toilet?	¿Puedo usar el baño? [pwedo oossar el banyo]
Could you give me the key for the toilet, please?	¿Me da la llave del baño, por favor? [meh da la yabeh del banyo, por fabor]
The toilet is blocked.	El baño está atascado (Am: tapado). [el banyo essta atasskado (tapado)]

clean	limpio [leemp-yo]
dirty	sucio [sooth-yo]
Gents (toilet for men)	Caballeros [kaba-yeross], Hombres [ombress]
Ladies (toilet for women)	Señoras [senyorass]
soap	el jabón [el khabon]

toilet paper	el papel higiénico [el papel eekh-yeneeko]
towel	toalla [to-a-ya]
washbasin	lavabo [lababo]

TRAVELLING WITH KIDS

Do you have children's portions?	¿Tienen ustedes también platos especiales para niños? [tyenen oosstedess tamb-yen platoss esspeth-yaless para neenyoss]
Could you warm up the bottle, please?	¿Me podría calentar el biberón, por favor? [meh podree-a kalentar el beeberon, por fabor]
Do you have a baby changing room?	¿Tiene algún cuarto para cambiar los pañales? [tyeneh algoon kwarto para kamb-yar loss pan-yaless]
Please bring another high chair.	Por favor, traiga otra silla alta para niño(s). [por fabor, trai-ga otra see-ya alta para neenyo(ss)]
armbands/water wings	los flotadores (de brazos) [loss flotadoress (deh brathoss)], los manguitos [loss mangeetoss]
baby changing table	la mesa para cambiar los pañales [la messa para kamb-yar loss panyaless]
baby food	el alimento para niños [el aleemento para neenyoss]
baby monitor	interfono de bebés [eenterfono deh bebess]
babysitter	el/la canguro [el/la kangooro], el/la babysitter [el/la babee-seeter]
bottle warmer	el calientabiberón [el kal-yenta-beeberon]
child discount	la reducción para niños [la redook-thyon para neenyoss]
child's safety seat	el asiento de seguridad para niños [el assyento deh segooreedad para neenyoss]
cot	cuna [koona]
day care	la guardería infantil [la gwarderee-a eemfanteel]
dummy	el chupete [el choopeteh]
feeding bottle	el biberón [el beeberon]
nappies/diapers	los pañales [loss panyaless]
paddling pool	piscina para niños [peess-theena para neenyoss]
playground	el parque infantil [el parkeh eemfanteel]
rubber ring	el flotador [el flotador]
toys	los juguetes [loss khoogetess]

Weather: page 19
Numbers: Inside front cover
Time: page 16, 17

THE MOST IMPORTANT WORDS

The numbers printed after some words are there to point you to the relevant page in a related chapter.

Abbreviations: adj = adjective; adv = adverb; n = noun; prep = preposition; v = verb; Am: = U.S. English/Latin American Spanish; Arg: = Argentinian Spanish; Br: = British English; sing = singular; pl = plural

A

a un m [oon], una f [oona]
abandon v abandonar [abandonar]
able: to be able to poder [poder]
about (approximately) aproximado [aproksseemado]; (time: e.g. about 7 pm) hacia [ath-ya]
absolutely sin falta [seen falta], absolutamente [abssolootamenteh]
accessible (for people with disabilities) adecuado para minusválidos [adekwado para meenooss-baleedoss]
accident el accidente [el aktheedenteh] ➤ 24; (to have an accident) sufrir un accidente [soofreer oon aktheedenteh]
accommodation alojamiento [alokha-mee-ento]
accompany acompañar [akompanyar]
activity la actividad [la akteebeedad]
activity holiday/vacation vacaciones pl, f activas [bakath-yoness akteebass] ➤ 85
additional suplementario [sooplementar-yo], adicional [adeeth-yonal]
address las señas [lass senyass], la dirección [la deerek-thyon] ➤ 114; (addressee) destinatario [dessteena-tar-yo] ➤ 114
adjust ajustar [akhoosstar], regular [regoolar]
adult n adulto [adoolto], adulta [adoolta]
advance (in advance) de antemano [deh antemano]; (advance booking) venta anticipada [benta anteetheepada] ➤ 83
advise v aconsejar [akonssekhar]
aeroplane (airplane) avión [ab-yon] ➤ 30
afraid: to be afraid of tener miedo de [tener mee-edo deh]
after después de [desspwess deh]
(in the) afternoon (por la) la tarde [(por la) tardeh]
again otra vez [otra beth], de nuevo [deh nwebo]
against contra [kontra]
age n la edad [la edad] ➤ 14
agency (office, bureau) agencia [akhenth-ya]
agree (consent to) consentir [konssenteer]; (come to an agreement) ponerse de acuerdo [ponersseh deh akwerdo]; (be in agreement) estar de acuerdo [esstar deh akwerdo]
air el aire [el ai-reh]
airport aeropuerto [ai-ro-pwerto]
alcohol level (blood) por mil [por meel]
all todo [todo], toda [toda]; pl todos los [todoss loss], todas las [todass lass]

allow permitir [permeeteer]
alone solo [solo]
along prep a lo largo de [a lo largo deh]
already ya [ya]
also también [tamb-yen]
altitude altura [altoora]
always siempre [syempreh]
ambulance ambulancia [amboolanth-ya]
American (man/woman) americano/americana [amereekano/amereekana]
among entre [entreh]; (among others) entre otros [entreh otross]
amount (money) el importe [el eemporteh], suma [sooma] ➤ 106
and y [ee]
Andalusian (man/woman) andaluz/andaluza [andalooth/andalootha]
angry enfadado [enfadado], furioso [fooree-osso]
animal el animal [el aneemal]
annoy molestar [molesstar], fastidiar [fassteed-yar]; (annoying) pesado [pessado], molesto [molessto]; (to be annoyed about/at) enfadarse por [emfadarsseh por];
another otro [otro]
apart from además [ademass], aparte de eso [aparteh deh esso]
apartment vivienda [beeb-yenda], piso [peesso], Am: departamento [departamento]
apologize disculparse [deesskoolparsseh], pedir perdón [pedeer perdon] ➤ 12
appetite apetito [apeteeto]
appointment (meeting) cita [theeta], fecha [fecha]; (deadline) plazo [platho]
area área [araya], la extensión [la ekss-ten-syon]
area code prefijo [prefeekho] ➤ 115
Argentinian (man/woman) argentino/argentina [arkhenteeno/arkenteena]
around prep alrededor de [alrededor deh], en torno a [en torno a]
arrival llegada [yegada] ➤ 30
arrive v llegar [yegar] ➤ 32
as far as I'm concerned por mi parte [por mee parteh]
as if como si [komo see]
ask (s.o. for sth) pedir (algo a alg) [pedeer (algo a alg-yen]
at (time) a [a]
at home en casa [en kassa]
at least por lo menos [por lo menoss], al menos [al menoss]

Atlantic Atlántico [atlanteeko]
attack v asaltar [assaltar], atracar [atrakar]
aunt tía [tee-a]
authorities (police, etc.) la autoridad pública [la owtoreedad poobleeka]
available (on sale) obtenible [obteneebleh], en venta [en benta]
average adj medio [med-yo], mediano [med-yano]; n medio [med-yo]; (on average) por término medio [por termeeno med-yo]
awake adj despierto [dess-pyerto]
away (gone) fuera [fwera], ausente [owssenteh]

B

baby el bebé [el bebeh] **>** 119
bachelor soltero [soltero]
back: to be back haber vuelto [aber vwelto]
bad adj malo [malo], mal [mal]
badly adv mal [mal]
baggage (luggage) el equipaje [el ekeepakheh] **>** 31
ball (sports) pelota [pelota]; (dance) el baile [el bai-leh]; (music) banda [banda], orquesta [orkessta]
bank banco [banko] **>** 104
bar el bar [el bar], taberna [taberna] **>** 39, 82
Basque (man/woman) vasco/vasca [bassko/basska]; (language) euskera [ayoosskera], vascuence [basskwentheh]
bathing/seaside resort la estación balnearia [la esstath-yom balnay-ar-ya]
bay (sea, etc.) bahía [ba-ee-a], golfo [golfo]
be v estar [esstar]
beach playa [pla-ya] **>** 84
beautiful hermoso [ermosso], bello [bayo], lindo [leendo]
because porque [porkeh], pues [pwess]; (because of) a causa de [a kowssa deh], por [por]
become v ponerse [ponersseh], hacerse [athersseh], llegar a ser [yegar a ser]
bed cama [kama]
bedroom la habitación [la abeetath-yon], Am: pieza [pyessa] **>** 6, 68
bee abeja [abekha]
before antes [antess], antes de [antess deh]
begin comenzar [komenthar]; (beginning) principio [preentheep-yo], comienzo [kom-yentho]
behind detrás de [detrass deh]
believe creer [kray-er]
bell timbre [teembreh]
belong v pertenecer [pertenether]; (belong to s.o.) pertenecer a alg [pertenether a alg-yen]
below debajo de [debakho deh]
bench banco [banko] **>** 111
bend (in a road, etc.) curva [koorba]
beside/by prep cerca de [therka deh]
between entre [entreh]
bicycle bicicleta [beetheekleta] **>** 23, 87
big grande [grandeh]
bill n (Am: the check) cuenta [kwenta], factura [faktoora] **>** 38, 71

birth nacimiento [nathee-mee-ento]; (birthday) el cumpleaños [el koomplay-anyoss] **>** 12; (birthplace) el lugar de nacimiento [el loogar deh nathee-mee-ento] **>** 22
bit: a bit un poco [oon poko]
bite v morder [morder]
black negro [negro]
blanket manta [manta]
blood la sangre [la sangreh] **>** 108
blue azul [athool]
boat barca [barka], el bote [el boteh], lancha [lancha] **>** 85
body cuerpo [kwerpo] **>** 109
boil v hervir [erbeer], cocer [kother]
book n libro [leebro]
booking reserva [resserba] **>** 6, 30, 83
border (international) frontera [frontera]; (boundary/limit) el límite [el leemeeteh] **>** 22
boring aburrido [abooreedo]
born nacido [natheedo]
boss n el jefe [el khefeh]
both ambos [amboss], los dos [loss doss]
bottle n botella [botaya]
bouquet ramo [ramo]
boy muchacho [moochacho], chico [cheeko]; (boyfriend) amigo [ameego], novio [nob-yo]
brakes n frenos [frenoss] **>** 24
brand n (i.e. brand name) marca [marka]
bread el pan [el pan] **>** 43, 46, 63
break v romper [romper]; (break into) violentar [bee-olentar] **>** 117
breakdown (car, etc.) avería [aberee-a] **>** 24, 25
breakfast desayuno [dessa-yoono] **>** 46, 70
brief adj breve [brebeh]
bring traer [tra-er], llevar [yebar]
broad ancho [ancho]
broken estropeado [esstropay-ado], roto [roto]
brother hermano [ermano]
brother-in-law cuñado [koonyado]
brushwood el matorral [el matoral]
building edificio [edeefeeth-yo]
bull toro [toro]
bureau de change cambio [kamb-yo] **>** 104
burn v quemar [kemar], incendiar [eenthend-yar]
bus el autobús [el owtobooss] **>** 34
bush, shrub mata [mata]
business days los días laborables [loss dee-ass laborabless]
but pero [pero]
buy v comprar [komprar]
by (i.e. written by) de [deh]
bye! adiós! [ad-yoss], hasta luego! [assta lwego]

C

cabin cabina [kabeena], el camarote [el kamaroteh] **>** 33
café el café [el kafeh]
calculate v calcular [kalkoolar]
calendar of events calendario de actos [kalendar-yo deh aktoss] **>** 82

call v llamar [yamar]; (name) nombrar [nombrar]; (on the phone) llamar por teléfono [yamar por telefono], telefonear [telefonay-ar]; (to be called) llamarse [yamarsseh]

calm n la paz [la path], la tranquilidad [la trankeeleedad]; (calm down) calmarse [kalmarsseh], tranquilizarse [trankee-leeth-arsseh]

camping el camping [el kampeeng] > 9, 76; (campsite) el camping [el kampeeng]

Canadian (man/woman) canadiense [kana-dyen-seh]

cancel anular [anoolar], cancelar [kanthelar]

capable: to be capable of ~ ser capaz de [ser kapath deh]

car el coche [el kocheh], el automóvil [el owtomobeel] > 23

care: take care of (of someone) cuidar de [kweedar deh], tener cuidado de [tener kweedado deh]; (deal with) ocuparse de [okooparsseh deh]

carry llevar [yebar]

cash dinero efectivo [deenero efektccbo], moneda contante [moneda kontanteh]

cash register caja [kakha]

cashpoint (ATM) cajero automático [kakhero owtomateeko] > 105

castanets las castañuelas [lass kasstan-ywelass]

Castilian (man/woman) castellano/castellana [kasstayano/kasstayana]; (language) castellano [kasstayano]

castle palacio [palath-yo], castillo [kasstee-yo] > 80

cat gato [gato]

Catalan (man/woman) el catalán/la catalana [el katalan/la katalana]; (language) (el) catalán [(el) katalan]

caution (care) prudencia [proodenth-ya], cautela [kowtela]

ceiling techo [techo]

celebration fiesta [fyessta]

cell phone (Br: mobile phone) teléfono móvil [telefono mobeel], Am: cedular [sedoolar] > 115

centre (Am: center) centro [thentro]

certain adj determinado [determeenado], cierto [th-yerto]

certainly adv seguro [segooro], ciertamente [th-yertamenteh]

certify certificar [therteefeekar]

chair silla [see-ya]

change n (coins) (las) monedas [(lass) monedass], dinero suelto [deenero swelto] > 106

change v cambiar [kamb-yar]; (money) cambiar [kamb-yar]; (trains, etc.) cambiar de [kamb-yar deh]

channel (TV) el canal [el kanal]

chapel capilla [kapee-ya] > 80

cheap barato [barato]

cheat v engañar [enganyar]

check n (Br: bill) cuenta [kwenta], factura [faktoora] > 38, 71; v controlar [kontrolar]

cheerful alegre [alegreh], de buen humor [deh bwen oomor]

cheese queso [kesso] > 43, 46, 63

chemist's/drug store droguería [drogeree-a] > 56, 58

cheque (Am: check) el cheque [el chekeh] > 105

child niño/niña [neenyo/neenya]

Chilean (man/woman) chileno/chilena [cheeleno/cheelena]

choose escoger [essko-kher], elegir [ele-kheer]

church iglesia [eeglessya] > 81

cigarette cigarrillo [theegaree-yo]

cinema el cine [el theeneh] > 82

city centre centro (de la ciudad) [thentro (deh la th-yoodad)]

city hall ayuntamiento [a-yoonta-mee-ento] > 80

clean adj limpio [leemp-yo]; v limpiar [leemp-yar]

clergyman/woman el pastor [el passtor], la pastora [la passtora]; (priest) el sacerdote m [el sather-doteh], la diaconisa f [la dyakoneessa]

clever (intelligent) inteligente [eentelee-khenteh], listo [leessto]

climate el clima [el kleema] > 19

climb v subir [soobeer]

clock el reloj (de pared) [el relokh (deh pared)]

closed cerrado [therado]

clothes ropa [ropa], los vestidos [loss bessteedoss] > 62

coast costa [kossta]

cockroach cucaracha [kookaracha]

coffee el café [el kafeh] > 46, 52

coin moneda [moneda]

cold adj frío [free-o]; (to be cold) tener/pasar frío [tener/passar free-o]

collect v coleccionar [kolek-thyonar]; (gather) recoger [reko-kher]

Colombian (man/woman) colombiano/colombiana [kolomb-yano/komob-yana]

colour n (Am: color) el color [el kolor] > 106

come v venir [beneer]; (come from) proceder [protheder], venir de [beneer deh]; (come in!) ¡adelante! [adelanteh], ¡pase! [passeh]

common adj común [komoon]

communication problems las dificultades de comprensión [lass deefeekool-tadess deh kompren-syon]

company (business) empresa [empressa]

compare v comparar [komparar], confrontar [komfrontar]

compensation la indemnización [la een-dem-nee-thath-yon]

complain (complain about) quejarse de [ke-kharsseh deh]; (formally) reclamar [reklamar] > 38, 70; (complaint) la reclamación [la reklamath-yon] > 38, 70

complete adj completo [kompleto]; (whole) entero [entero]; (finished) terminado [termeenado]

completely adv completamente [kompletamenteh], del todo [del todo]

compliments cumplidos m [koompleedoss] > 13

computer el ordenador [el ordenador] > 59

computer shop/store tienda de informática [tyenda deh eemformateeka] > 56, 59

concert concierto [konth-yerto] > 83

concierge (porter) portero [portero]

condom preservativo [presserbateebo], el condón [el kondon]
confirm confirmar [komfeermar]
confiscate confiscar [komfeesskar]
confuse confundir [komfoondeer]
congratulate felicitar [feleetheetar]; (congratulations) la felicitación [la feleetheetath-yon], enhorabuena [enora-bwena] ➤ 12
connect (technology, etc.) conectar [konektar]; (on the telephone) poner en comunicación [poner en komooneekath-yon]
connection (personal) la relación [la relath-yon], contacto [kontakto]; (travel) el empalme [el empalmeh] ➤ 30, 32
constitution (political) la constitución [la konsstee-tooth-yon]
consulate consulado [konssoolado]
contact n contacto [kontakto]; v contactar [kontaktar], ponerse en contacto [ponersseh en kontakto]
contents contenido [konteneedo]
continue continuar [konteen-war]
contraceptive n anticonceptivo [antee-konthep-teebo]
contract contrato [kontrato]
conversation la conversación [la komber-sath-yon]
cook v cocinar [kotheenar]
cool (temp.) fresco [fressko]
corner (outer) esquina [esskeena]; (inner) el rincón [el reenkon]
corridor corredor [koredor]
corrupt corrompido [korompeedo]
cost v costar [kosstar], valer [baler]
Costa Rican (man/woman) costarricense [kosstaree-thensseh]
counter (post office, etc.) la ventanilla [la bentanee-ya], Am: boletería [boleteree-a]
country (nation) el país [el pa-eess]; (home/native country) patria [patree-a]
country estate finca rústica [feenka roossteeka], Am: finca rural [feenka rooral]; (country house) casa de campo [kassa deh kampo]
couple (married) matrimonio [matreemonyo], pareja [parekha]
course (lessons) curso [koorsso]; (meal) plato [plato]
court (law) el tribunal [el treeboonal] ➤ 118
cousin el primo m [el preemo], la prima f [la preema]
credit card tarjeta de crédito [tarkheta deh kredeeto] ➤ 54, 71, 106
criticize v criticar [kreeteekar]
cross v (a road, etc.) cruzar [kroothar], atravesar [atrabessar]
cry (weep) llorar [yorar]
Cuban (man/woman) cubano/cubana [koobano/koobana]
culture cultura [kooltoora] ➤ 80
curious curioso [koor-yosso]
currency moneda [moneda] ➤ 106
current (electrical) la corriente [la kor-yenteh]
cushion el cojín [el kokheen]
customs (border control) aduana [adwana] ➤ 22

D

damage n daño [danyo]; v dañar [danyar]
damaged (faulty, defective) averiado [aber-yado] ➤ 24
dance bailar [bai-lar] ➤ 82; (dance hall) sala de baile [sala deh baileh] ➤ 82
dangerous peligroso [peleegrosso]
dark oscuro [osskooro]
date (appointment) cita [theeta], compromiso [kompromeesso]; (calendar) fecha [fecha] ➤ 17; (date of birth) fecha de nacimiento [fecha deh nathee-mee-ento] ➤ 22
daughter hija [eekha]
day el día [el dee-a]; (day of arrival) el día de llegada [el dee-a deh yegada]
dead muerto [mwerto]
dear adj (friend, etc.) querido [kereedo]
death la muerte [la mwerteh]
debt deuda [dayooda]
decide decidir [detheedeer], decidirse [detheedeersseh]
decision la decisión [la detheessyon], la resolución [la ressolooth-yon]
declare declarar [deklarar]
deep profundo [profoondo], hondo [ondo]; (low) bajo [bakho]
definite adj definitivo [defeenee-teebo]
definitely adv definitivamente [defeenee-teeba-menteh]
degree (temperature, etc.) grado [grado]
demand v pedir [pedeer], exigir [ek-see-kheer]
denomination (relig.) la religión [la relee-khyon], la confesión religiosa [la komfessyon relee-khyossa]
dentist el/la dentista [el/la denteessta] ➤ 108
departure salida [saleeda], partida [parteeda] ➤ 32, 34
deposit (security deposit) fianza [fyantha], la caución [la kowth-yon]
deserve merecer [merether]
destination meta de(l) viaje [meta deh/(del) bee-akheh]
destroy destruir [desstroo-eer]
details (personal details) los datos personales [loss datoss perssonaless]
develop v desarrollar [dessaroyar]; (photos) revelar [rebelar]
dial v (phone number) marcar [markar] ➤ 115
die v morir [moreer]
difference diferencia [deeferenth-ya]
different adj distinto [deessteento], diferente [deeferenteh]
differently adv de otra manera/forma [deh otra manera/forma]
difficult difícil [deefeetheel]
direction la dirección [la deerekth-yon]
director (manager) el director [el deerektor]
directory n lista [leessta], catálogo [katalogo]

dirt n la suciedad [la sooth-yedad]

dirty adj sucio [sooth-yo]

disabled toilets lavabo para minusválidos [lababo para meenooss-baleedoss]

disappointed desilusionado [dessee-loo-syon-ado]

disco discoteca [deesskoteka] > 82

discount rebaja [rebakha], descuento [desskwento]

discover descubrir [desskoobreer]

distance trayecto [tra-yekto], trecho [trecho]

distant (far away) distante [deesstanteh], alejado [alekhado]

distrust v desconfiar [desskom-fee-ar]

disturb molestar [molesstar], estorbar [esstorbar]; (disturbance) molestia [molesstya], estorbo [esstorbo]

diversion la desviación [la dess-bee-ath-yon]

dizzy mareado [maray-ado]; (dizziness) vértigo [berteego]

do v hacer [ather]

doctor médico m [medeeko], médica f [medeeka] > 107

dog perro [pero]

donkey burro [booro], asno [azno]

door puerta [pwerta]

double doble [dobleh]

doubt sth dudar de algo [doodar deh algo]

downwards hacia abajo [ath-ya abakho]

dream v soñar [sonyar]

dress (a wound) v vendar [bendar]; (dressing) el vendaje [el benda-kheh]

drink n bebida [bebeeda] > 45, 52, 53; v beber [beber], tomar [tomar]

drive v conducir [kondootheer], Am: manejar [manekhar]

driving licence permiso/el carné de conducir [permeesso/el karneh deh kondootheer]; (driving documents) la documentación de coche [la dokoomen-tath-yon deh kocheh]

drunk borracho [boracho], Am: apimpado [apeem-pado]; (tipsy) alegre [alegreh], bebido [bebeedo], Am: alegrón [alegron]; (get drunk) emborracharse [embora-charsseh]

duration la duración [la doorath-yon]

during durante [dooranteh]

duty la obligación [la obleegath-yon], el deber [el deber]

■ ■ E

early temprano [temprano]

earn v ganar [ganar]

earth tierra [tyera]

east el este [el essteh]

easy fácil [fatheel]

eat comer [komer]

Ecuadorian (man/woman) ecuatoriano/ecuatoriana [ekwator-yano/ekwator-yana]

edge n orilla [oree-ya], el borde [el bordeh]

edible comestible [komessteebleh]

education la educación [la edookath-yon]

effort (trouble) esfuerzo [essfwertho]

egg huevo [webo]

either... or o ... o ... [o ... o ...]

electrical shop (tienda de) artículos eléctricos [(tyenda deh)arteekooloss elektreekoss] > 56, 59

elevator el ascensor [el ass-thenssor]

email address correo electrónico [korayo elektroneeko] > 8

embassy embajada [embakhada]

emergency brake freno de alarma [freno deh alarma] > 32

emergency exit salida de emergencia [saleeda deh emerkhenth-ya] > 30

emergency telephone el poste de socorro [el possteh deh sokoro] > 27

emphasis énfasis m [enfassees], acento [athento]

employment empleo [emplayo]

empty vacío [bathee-o]

end v terminar [termeenar], acabar [akabar]

engaged: to get engaged to prometerse con [prometersseh kon]

engine (motor) el motor [el motor] > 24, 27

England Inglaterra [eenglatera]

English (language) inglés [eengless]; (Englishman/woman) el inglés/la inglesa [el eengless/la eenglessa]

enjoy v gozar de [gothar deh], disfrutar de [deessfrootar deh]

enough bastante [basstanteh], suficiente [soofeeth-yenteh]

enquire informarse [eemformarsseh]

enter entrar en [entrar en]; (a country) entrar en el país [entrar en el pa-eess]

entertainment divertimiento [deebertee-mee-ento], la diversión [la deeberssyon] > 82; (entertaining) divertido [deeberteedo]

entrance n entrada [entrada]

environment el (medio) ambiente [el (med-yo) amb-yenteh]

et cetera etcétera [et-theh-tera]

Euro euro [ayooro] > 104

Europe Europa [ayoo-ro-pa]

European (man/woman) europeo/europea [ayoo-ro-payo/ayoo-ro-paya]

even adv hasta [assta]

evening (before dark) la tarde [la tardeh]; (after dark) la noche [la nocheh]

event (occurrence) acontecimiento [akontethee-mee-ento], suceso [soothesso]; (performance, show) espectáculo [esspek-takoolo] > 83

every cada [kada], todos [todoss]; (every time) cada vez [kada beth], siempre [syempreh]

everyone todo el mundo [todo el moondo]

everything todo [todo]

everywhere por/en todas partes [por/en todass partess]

evil malo [malo]

exact adj exacto [ekssakto], preciso [pretheesso]

exactly adv exactamente [ekssaktamenteh]

examination (inspection) el examen [el ekssamen]

examine examinar [ekssameenar], controlar [kontrolar]

example ejemplo [ekhemplo]

except (apart from) excepto [ekss-thepto]

exchange cambiar [kamb-yar]; (exchange rate) cambio [kamb-yo] ➤ 106

excuse n excusa [ekss-koossa]

exhausted agotado [agotado]

exit n salida [saleeda]; (motorway/highway) salida de autopista [saleeda deh owtopeessta]

expenses los gastos [loss gasstoss]

expensive caro [karo]

experienced adj experimentado [ek-spereementado]

expire (voucher, etc.) caducar [kadookar], vencer [benther]

explain explicar [eksspleekar], aclarar [aklarar]

extend v alargar [alargar]; (time) prolongar [prolongar]

extinguish apagar [apagar]

F

factory fábrica [fabreeka]

faith la fe [la feh]; (faithful) fiel [fyel]

fall v caer [ka-er]

family familia [fameel-ya]

far (distance) largo [largo]; (far away) lejano [lekhano]

farewell: say farewell despedirse [desspedeerseh] ➤ 12

fashion moda [moda] ➤ 62

fast-food restaurant cafetería [kafeteree-a], el bar [el bar]; (on the beach) chiringuito [cheereengeeto]

fat adj gordo [gordo]; (swollen) hinchado [eenchado]; n graso [grasso], gordo [gordo]

father el padre [el padreh]

fear n miedo [mee-edo]; v temer [temer]

fee tarifa [tareefa]; (professional charges) los honorarios [loss onor-ar-yoss]

feel v, **feeling** n sentir [senteer], sentimiento [sentee-mee-ento]

feminine femenino [femeneeno]

festival fiesta [fyessta]

few poco [poko]; (a few) un par de [oon par deh]

fiancé/fiancée el prometido [el prometeedo], la prometida [la prometeeda]

field campo [kampo]

fill in/out (a form, etc.) completar [kompletar], llenar [yenar]

film (movie) película para el cine [peleekoola para el theene]; (for a camera) película [peleekoola], el film(e) [el feel-m(eh)]

finally finalmente [feenalmenteh]

find v encontrar [enkontrar]

fine (financial penalty) multa [moolta]

finish v terminar [termeenar]; (finished) terminado [termeenado]

fire alarm el avisador de incendios [el abeessador deh eenthend-yoss]

fire extinguisher el extintor [el ekss-teentor]

fire n fuego [fwego]; (building, forest, etc.) incendio [eenthend-yo]

fire service los bomberos [loss bombeross]

firewood leña [lenya]

first aid los primeros auxilios [loss pree-meross owk-seel-yoss]

first floor (Br: ground floor) piso bajo [peesso bakho], Am: los bajos [loss bakhoss]

first name el nombre (de pila) [el nombreh (deh peela)] ➤ 22

firstly (first of all) primero [preemero], en primer lugar [en preemer loogar]

fish n (alive) el pez [el peth]; (as food) el pescado [el pesskado] ➤ 45, 48

fishmonger el pescadero [el pesskadero], la pescadera [la pesskadera]

flash (photo) el flash [el flass]

flat adj llano [yano]

flaw (personality, etc.) defecto [defekto]

flight vuelo [bwelo] ➤ 31

flirt v coquetear [koketay-ar] ➤ 15

floor piso [peesso]

flow v correr [korer]

flower la flor [la flor]

fly volar [bolar]; (plane) ir en avión [eer en ab-yon]; n (animal) mosca [mosska]

follow seguir [segeer]

food los comestibles [loss komessteebless] ➤ 41, 63

for para [para], por [por]

forbid v prohibir [pro-eebeer]

forbidden adj prohibido [pro-eebeedo]

foreign extranjero [ekss-tran-khero]; (foreigner) extranjero [ekss-tran-khero], extranjera [ekss-tran-khera]

forest el bosque [el bosskeh] ➤ 81

forget olvidar [olbeedar]

forgive disculpar [deesskoolpar], perdonar [perdonar]

fork el tenedor [el tenedor]

form (to fill in) impreso [eempresso], formulario [formoolar-yo] ➤ 106

fragile frágil [frakheel]

free (of charge) gratuito [gratweeto], gratis [grateess]

freeze (water) helar [elar]; (food) congelar [konkhelar]

frequently adv frecuentemente [frekwentementeh], a menudo [a menoodo]

fresh fresco [fressko]

friend el amigo [el ameego], la amiga [la ameega]; (friendly) amable [amableh]; (to be friends) ser amigo (with = de) [ser ameego (deh)]

frighten asustar [assoo-star]; (to be frightened) estar asustado [esstar assoo-stado]

from (origin) de [deh]; (time) de [deh], desde [dezdeh]

front: in front of delante de [delanteh deh]

fruit fruta [froota] ➤ 42, 46, 51, 63

full lleno [yeno], completo [kompleto]

full (after food) harto [arto], satisfecho [sateessfecho]

full board (accommodation) la pensión completa [la penssyon kompleta] ➤ 70, 72

fun la diversión [la deeberssyon]

furious rabioso [rab-yosso], furioso [foor-yosso]

furniture el mueble [el mweh-bleh]

fuse (electric) el fusible [el foosseebleh]

Galician (man/woman) gallego/gallega [ga-yego/ga-yega]; (language) gallego [ga-yego]
garage (for repairs) taller m de reparaciones [ta-yer deh reparath-yoness]; (car storage) el garaje [el garakheh]
garbage n (Br: rubbish) basura [bassoora]
garden el jardín [el khardeen]
gas (Br: petrol) gasolina [gassoleena], Arg: nafta [nafta] **> 23**
gas station (Br: petrol station) gasolinera [gassoleenera], la estación de servicio [la esstath-yon deh serbeeth-yo] **> 23, 28**
gear (on a car, etc.) marcha [marcha]
gentleman el señor [el senyor]
genuine verdadero [berdadero], auténtico [owtenteeko]
get (obtain) procurar [prokoorar], proporcionar [proporth-yonar]
get out (of a bus, etc.) bajar [bakhar] **> 32, 34**
get up levantarse [lebantarsseh]
gift (present) regalo [regalo]
girl muchacha [moochacha], chica [cheeka]; (girlfriend) amiga [ameega], novia [nob-ya]
give dar [dar]; (as a gift) regalar [regalar]
give up: to give up (seat) ceder [theder]; (habit) dejar [dekhar]
gladly! (with pleasure!) ¡con gusto! [kon goossto], ¡de buena gana! [deh bwena gana]
glass (for drinking) vaso [basso], copa [kopa]; (material) el cristal [el kreesstal], vidrio [beedree-o]
glasses (spectacles) las gafas [lass gafass], Am: los lentes [loss lentess] **> 65**
go ir [eer]
goal (aim) meta [meta]
God Dios [dee-oss]
good bueno [bweno], buen [bwen]
goodbye: to say goodbye despedirse [dess-ped-eer-seh]
government gobierno [gob-yerno]
grandeur lo imponente [lo eemponenteh]
grandfather, grandmother el abuelo [el abwelo], la abuela [la abwela]
grandson, granddaughter el nieto [el nyeto], la nieta [la nyeta]
gratuity (Br: tip) propina [propeena] **> 35, 40**
grave (tomb) tumba [toomba]
green verde [berdeh]
greet saludar [saloodar]
grey gris [greess]
ground (earth) suelo [swelo]
ground floor (Am: first floor) piso bajo [peesso bakho], Am: los bajos [loss bakhoss]
group grupo [groopo]
guarantee garantía [garantee-a]
Guatemalan (man/woman) guatemalteco/ gualtemalteca [gwatemalteko/gwaltemalteka]
guess v adivinar [adeebeenar]
guest invitado/invitada [eenbeetado/eenbeetada]; (hotel guest) el huésped [el wessped]

guesthouse la pensión [la penssyon], fonda [fonda], posada [possada] **> 8, 68**
guide (book) la guía (turística) [la gee-a (tooreessteeka)] **> 67**
guided tour visita guiada [beesseeta gyada] **> 79**
guilt culpa [koolpa]
guitar guitarra [geetara]

hair pelo [pelo] **> 60**
hairdresser's (for women) peluquería de señoras [pelookeree-a deh senyorass]; (for men) peluquería de caballeros [pelookeree-a deh kaba-yeross] **> 56, 60**
half medio [med-yo]
hall (large room) sala [sala]
handwriting escritura [esskreetoora]
happen pasar [passar], suceder [sootheder], ocurrir [okoorreer]
happy contento [kontento], feliz [feleeth], dichoso [deechosso]; (satisfied) satisfecho [sateessfecho]
hard (solid) duro [dooro]; (difficult) difícil [deefeetheel]
hardly apenas [apenass]
harmful nocivo [notheebo], dañino [danyeeno]
have (possess) tener [tener]; (have to) deber [deber], tener que [tener keh]
he él [el]
health la salud [la salood];
healthy sano [sano]
hear v oír [o-eer]
heating la calefacción [la kalefak-thyon] **> 70**
heaven cielo [th-yelo]
heavy pesado [pessado]
hello! ¡hola! [ola]; (on the phone) ¡hola! [ola], ¡diga! [deega]
help n ayuda [a-yooda]; v ayudar [a-yoodar]
her su [soo]
here aquí [akee]
high alto [alto]
hike v hacer excursiones a pie [ather ekss-koor-syoness a pyeh] **> 88**
hill colina [koleena]
hire alquilar [alkeelar] **> 29, 77**
his su [soo]
history historia [eesstor-ya]
hobby la afición [la afeeth-yon], el hobby [el obbee]
hold v sujetar [sookhetar]
hole agujero [agookhero]; (puncture) pinchazo [peenchatho]
holiday home casa de vacaciones [kassa deh bakath-yoness] **> 9, 74**
holiday (Am: vacation) las vacaciones [lass bakath-yoness]
holy santo [santo], sagrado [sagrado]
home-made casero [kassero]
Honduran (man/woman) hondureño/hondureña [ondoorenyo/ondoorenya]
hope v esperar [essperar]
hospital el hospital [el osspeetal], clínica [kleeneeka] **> 108**

host/hostess el anfitrión [el amfeetree-on], la anfitriona [la amfeetree-ona]

hot muy caliente [mwee kal-yenteh]

hotel el hotel [el otel] ➤ 6, 68

hour hora [ora]

house casa [kassa]

household goods los artículos domésticos [loss arteekooloss domesteekoss]

how? cómo [komo]; **(how long?)** ¿cuánto tiempo? [kwanto tyempo]; **(how many?)** ¿cuántos? [kwantoss]; **(how much?)** ¿cuánto? [kwanto]

however pero [pero], sin embargo [seen embargo]

hug v abrazar [abrathar]

hunger n el hambre [el ambreh]; **(hungry)** hambriento [ambree-ento]

hurt v doler [doler]

husband esposo [essposso], marido [mareedo]

I yo [yo]

idea idea [eedaya]

identity card (ID) tarjeta [tarkheta], el carné/documento de identidad [el karneh/dokoomento deh eedenteedad], Am: cédula personal [sedoola perssonal]

if si [see]

ill (Am: sick) enfermo [emfermo] ➤ 106

illness la enfermedad [la enfermedad]

immediately immediatamente [eem-med-yata-menteh], enseguida [en-segeeda], Am: ahorita [a-oreeta]

impolite descortés [desskortess], mal educado [mal edookado]

import n la importación [la eemportath-yon] ➤ 22

important importante [eemportanteh]

impossible imposible [eemposseebleh]

in en [en]

in addition además [ademass]

included (in the price, etc.) incluido [eenkloo-eedo]

inform informar [eemformar]; **(advise/warn)** avisar [abeessar]

information la información [la eemformath-yon]

information office/bureau oficina de información [ofeetheena deh eemformath-yon]

inhabitant el habitante [el abeetanteh]

innocent inocente [eenothenteh]

insect insecto [eenssekto]

inside dentro [dentro]

inspect (check) comprobar [komprobar]

instead of en vez de [en beth deh], en lugar de [en loogar deh]

insult v ofender [ofender]

insurance seguro [segooro]

interested: to be interested (in) interesarse (por) [eenter-ess-ar-sseh (por)]

international internacional [eenternath-yonal]

Internet el internet [el eenternet]

interrupt v interrumpir [eenteroompeer]

interruption la interrupción [la eenteroopth-yon]

introduction (person) la presentación [la pressentath-yon]

invalid (void) inválido [eembaleedo]

invite v invitar [eembeetar]

invoice amount (billing amount) el importe de la factura [el eemporteh deh la faktoora]

Ireland, Eire Irlanda [eerlanda]

Irish(man/woman) el irlandés/irlandesa [el eerlandess/eerlandessa]

island isla [eezla]

isn't it? ¿(no es) verdad? [(no ess) berdad]

jellyfish medusa [medoossa]

jewellery las joyas [lass khoyass] ➤ 65

job (position) empleo [emplayo]

joke broma [broma], el chiste [el cheessteh]

journey el viaje [el bee-akheh]; **(return journey)** el viaje de vuelta [el bee-akheh deh bwelta]

joy alegría [alegree-a]

judge v juzgar [khooth-gar]

jungle selva [selba]

just (a moment ago) hace un momento [atheh oon momento], ahora mismo [a-ora meezmo]

just as... (good) as tan ... (bueno) como [tan ... (bweno) komo]

keep v guardar [gwardar], conservar [konsserbar]; **(a promise, etc.)** cumplir [koompleer]

key n la llave [la yabeh] ➤ 70, 72, 74

kind adj amable [amableh]; **(kindness)** la amabilidad [la ama-beelee-dad]

kiss n beso [besso]; v besar [bessar]

kitchen cocina [kotheena]

knife cuchillo [koochee-yo]

know conocer [konother]; **(get to know s.o.)** conocer a alguien [konother a alg-yen]

lack defecto [defekto]

ladder escalera [esskalera]

lady señora [senyora]

lake lago [lago]

land (ground) tierra [tyera]

landlord, lady dueño [dwenyo], dueña [dwenya]; el patrón [el patron], la patrona [la patrona]; propietario/propietaria (de la casa) [prop-yetar-yo/prop-yetar-ya (deh la kassa)] ➤ 74

landscape el paisaje [el pa-eesakheh] ➤ 81

language el idioma [el eed-yoma], lengua [lengwa]

large grande [grandeh]

last v durar [doorar]; adj último [oolteemo]

late tarde [tardeh]; **(to be late)** retrasarse [retrass-ar-seh], llegar tarde [yegar tardeh]

later adj posterior [possteree-or], ulterior [oolteree-or]; adv más tarde [mass tardeh]

laugh v reír(se) [ray-eer(seh)]

lawn el césped [el thessped], Arg: pasto [passto]

lazy perezoso [pereth-osso], holgazán [olgathan]

learn aprender [aprender]

leave partir (para) [parteer (para)], salir [saleer]; (hit the road) ponerse en camino [ponersseh en kameeno]

left: on the left a la izquierda [a la eeth-kyerda]

lend prestar [prestar], dejar [dekhar]; (to borrow) pedir prestado [pedeer presstado]

length (measure, distance) la longitud [la lonkheetood], la distancia [la deesstanth-ya]

less menos [menoss]

let (allow) dejar [dekhar]

letter (mail) carta [karta] > 114

lie down echarse [echarsseh], acostarse [akoss-tarsseh]

lie n (untruth) mentira [menteera]

life vida [beeda]

lifeboat el bote salvavidas [el boteh sal-ba-bee-dass] > 34

lift (Am: elevator) el ascensor [el ass-thenssor]

light n la luz [la looth]; adj (bright) claro [klaro]; adj (weight) ligero [leekhero], Am: liviano [leeb-yano]

lightning relámpago [relampago], el flash [el flass]

like v gustar [goosstar]

line (Br: queue) fila [feela]

listen escuchar [esskoochar]

little pequeño [pekenyo]; (a little bit of) un poco de … [oon poko deh]

live v vivir [beebeer]; (reside) habitar [abeetar]

located: to be located encontrarse [enkontrarsseh]

location la localización [la lokaleethath-yon]

lock n cerradura [theradoora]; v cerrar con llave [therar kon yabeh]

lodge (chalet) cabaña [kabanya], Am: bohío [bo-ee-o]

lone/lonely solo [solo], solitario [soleetar-yo]

long largo [largo]

long-distance call llamada interurbana/ de larga distancia [yamada eenteroorbana/deh larga deesstanth-ya] > 115

look after (take care of) tener cuidado (de/con) [tener kweedado (deh/kon)]

look out! ¡cuidado! [kweedado], ¡atención! [atenth-yon]

look v mirar [meerar]; (look for) buscar [boosskar]

lorry el camión [el kam-yon]

lose v perder [perder] > 118

loss n pérdida [perdeeda]

lost property office oficina de objetos perdidos [ofeetheena deh ob-khetoss perdeedoss] > 113

lost: to get lost v extraviarse [ekss-tra-bee-ar-sseh]

lot: a lot of mucho [moocho]

loud alto [alto]

loudspeaker el altavoz [el altaboth], Am: el altoparlante [el altoparlanteh]

love v amar [amar], querer [kerer]

low bajo [bakho]

low season temporada baja [temporada bakha] > 72

luck la felicidad [la feleetheedad]

lucky afortunado [afortoonado]

luggage (baggage) el equipaje [el ekeepakheh] > 31

lunch comida [komeeda], almuerzo [almwertho] > 40

■ M ■

machine máquina [makeena]

made from (material) de [deh]

magazine revista [rebeessta] > 67

maiden name el nombre de soltera [el nombreh deh soltera] > 22

mail v (post) enviar [emb-yar] > 114

mainland tierra firme [tyera feermeh]

make up one's mind decidirse [detheedeersseh]

make v hacer [ather]; (construct) fabricar [fabreekar]; (make tea/coffee) hacer el té/café [ather el teh/kafeh]

male masculino [masskooleeno]

man hombre [ombreh]

manager el jefe [el khefeh], la jefa [la khefa]; el director [el deerektor], la directora [la deerektora]

map el mapa [el mapa] > 67; (of a town/city) plano de la ciudad [plano deh la th-yoodad] > 67, 78; (walking/hiking) el mapa de excursiones [el mapa deh ekss-koor-syon-ess] > 67

market mercado [merkado] > 56, 81

marriage matrimonio [matreemonyo]

married (to) casado (con) [kassado (kon)]

marry casarse [kassarsseh]

mass (relig.) misa [meessa]

material tela [tela]

matter n asunto [assoonto]

maybe quizá(s) [keetha(ss)], tal vez [tal beth]

me me [meh]; (to me) a mí [a mee]

meal comida [komeeda] > 36, 63; (course, dish) plato [plato] > 38, 40, 46

mean v (signify) significar [seegneefeekar]

measurements las medidas [lass medeedass]

meat la carne [la karneh] > 44, 49

medicine medicina [medeetheena], medicamento [medeekamento] > 57, 60, 107

Mediterranean Sea (mar) Mediterráneo [(mar) medeeterranayo]

meet encontrar [enkontrar]

memorise memorizar [memoreezar]

menu el menú [el menoo] > 38, 46

message noticia [noteeth-ya], aviso [abeesso]

Mexican (man/woman) mexicano/mexicana [me-khee-kano/me-khee-kana]

middle medio [med-yo], centro [thentro]

minus menos [menoss]

minute n minuto [meenooto]

misfortune desgracia [dessgrath-ya]

Miss (title) señorita [senyoreeta]

miss v (a bus, etc.) perder [perder]; (someone, etc.) extrañar [ekss-tranyar]

mistake el error [el eror]; (by mistake) por equivocación [por ekeebo-kath-yon]; (to be mistaken) equivocarse [ekeebo-karsseh]

misunderstand entender mal [entender mal], interpretar mal [eenterpretar mal]

mixed mezclado [methklado]

mobile phone (Am: cell phone) teléfono móvil [telefono mobeel], Am: cedular [thedoolar] > 115

modern moderno [moderno]

moment momento [momento], el instante [el eensstanteh]

money dinero [deenero] ➤ 106

month el mes [el mess] ➤ 17

moon n luna [loona]

more más [mass]

morning mañana [manyana]; [in the morning] por la mañana [por la manyana]

mosquito mosquito [mosskeeto]

mother la madre [la madreh]

motive (reason, cause) motivo [moteebo]

motor (engine) el motor [el motor] ➤ 24, 27

motorbike la moto(cicleta) [la moto(theekleta)] ➤ 23

mountain montaña [montanya]; [mountain range] sierra [syera]

move house mudarse de casa [moodarsseh deh kassa]

movie película para el cine [peleekoola para el theeneh]

Mr/Mrs don/doña [don/donya]

mud barro [baro]

museum museo [moossayo] ➤ 79

music música [mooseeka]

my mi [mee]

N

naked desnudo [deznoodo]

name el nombre [el nombreh] ➤ 11

nation la nación [la nath-yon]

nationality la nacionalidad [la nath-yonaleedad]

natural adj natural [natooral]

nature naturaleza [natooraletha]

nausea las náuseas [lass now-sayass] ➤ 111

near adj cercano [therkano]; adv junto a [khoonto a], cerca de [therka deh]

nearby cerca [therka]

necessary necesario [nethessar-yo]

need v necesitar [nethesseetar]

neighbour vecino [betheeno], vecina [betheena]

neither tampoco [tampoko]

nephew sobrino [sobreeno]

nervous nervioso [nerb-yosso]

never nunca [noonka]

nevertheless sin embargo [seen embargo]

new nuevo [nwebo]

news las noticias [lass noteeth-yass]

newsagent's, news stand quiosco [kyossko]

newspaper periódico [per-yodeeko] ➤ 67

next próximo [prokseemo], siguiente [seeg-yenteh]; [next to] junto a [khoonto a], al lado de [al lado deh]

Nicaraguan (man/woman) nicaragüense [neek-ar-ag-wen-seh]

nice bonito [boneeto], lindo [leendo]

niece sobrina [sobreena]

night la noche [la nocheh]; [spend the night] pernoctar [pernoktar] ➤ 6, 68

night club el club nocturno [el kloob noktoorno] ➤ 82

nobody nadie [nad-yeh]

noise ruido [rweedo]

none/no ninguno [neengoono], ningún [neengoon]

noon el mediodía [el med-yo-dee-a]; [at noon] a(l) mediodía [a(l) med-yo-dee-a]

normal normal [normal]

north el norte [el norteh]

not no [no]; [no way/not at all] de ninguna manera [deh neengoona manera]; [not even] ni siquiera [nee seek-yera]

nothing nada [nada]

now ahora [a-ora]

nowhere en ninguna parte [en neengoona parteh]

number número [noomero]

nurse enfermero [emfermero], enfermera [emfermera]

O

object n objeto [obkheto]

observe (the rules) observar [obsserbar], tener en cuenta [tener en kwenta]

obtain obtener [obtener], conseguir [konssegeer]

occasion la ocasión [la okassyon]

occupied ocupado [okoopado]

ocean océano [othayano]

of de [deh]

of course adv naturalmente [natooralmenteh], Am: ¡cómo no! [komo no]

offend ofender [ofender]

offer v ofrecer [ofrether]

office oficina [ofeetheena]

often frecuentemente [frekwentementeh], a menudo [a menoodo]

oil el aceite [el a-thay-teh]

old viejo [bee-ekho]; [former, ancient] antiguo [anteegwo]

on prep sobre [sobreh], en [en], por [por]

on the contrary! ¡sí! [see], Am: ¿cómo no? [komo no]

once (one time) una vez [oona beth]

one (number) uno [oono]; (pronoun) se [seh], uno [oono]

only solo [solo], solamente [solamenteh]

open adj abierto [ab-yerto]; v abrir [abreer]

opening hours horas de apertura [orass deh apertoora]

opinion la opinión [la opeenyon]

opportunity la oportunidad [la oportooneedad]

oppose sth estar en contra de [esstar en kontra deh]

opposite opuesto [opwessto], contrario [kontrar-yo]; [the opposite] lo contrario [lo kontrar-yo]; [on the contrary] al contrario [al kontrar-yo]

optician óptico [opteeko] ➤ 56, 65

or o [o]

order n pedido [pedeedo] ➤ 38

organs: (internal) organs los órganos (internos) [loss organoss [eenternoss]]

origin (place of) lugar m de origen [loogar deh oreekhen] ➤ 14

other: the other el otro [el otro]

our nuestro [nwesstro], nuestra [nwesstra]

out of order fuera de servicio [fwera deh serbeeth-yo]

outside/outdoors fuera [fwera], afuera [afwera]

oven n horno [orno]

over sobre [sobreh]

overseas (el) ultramar [(el) ooltramar]

overtake adelantar [adelantar], pasar [passar]

owe v deber [deber]

own v poseer [possay-er]

owner propietario [prop-yet-ar-yo], proprietaria [prop-yet-ar-ya]

P

pack v hacer [ather]

package (small) paquetito [paketeeto]

page página [pakheena]

pain el dolor [el dolor], pena [pena]

painting n pintura [peentoora], cuadro [kwadro]

pair: a pair un par [oon par]

Panamanian (man/woman) panameño/panameña [panamenyo/panamenya]

papers (official documents) documentos [dokoomentoss] ➤ 28

Paraguayan (man/woman) paraguayo/paraguaya [paragwa-yo/paragwa-ya]

parcel el paquete [el paketeh] ➤ 114

pardon? sorry? ¡¿cómo?! [komo], ¿perdón? [perdon]

parents los padres [loss padress]

park v aparcar [aparkar] ➤ 23; n el parque [el parkeh]

part (piece) la parte [la parteh]

pass (mountain) paso [passo], puerto [pwerto]

passage paso [passo], pasaje m [passakheh]

passenger pasajero [passakhero], pasajera [passakhera]

passing through (in transit) de paso [deh passo]

passport el pasaporte [el passaporteh] ➤ 22, 116

passport control el control de pasaportes [el kontrol deh passaportess] ➤ 22

past (the past) pasado [passado]; (go past) por delante de [por delanteh deh]

path sendero [sendero], senda [senda]

pay v pagar [pagar]; (pay in cash) pagar al contado [pagar al kontado]

payment pago [pago]

peace la paz [la path]

people la gente [la khenteh]; (the people, citizens) pueblo [pweblo]

per por [por]; (per head) por cabeza [por kabetha]

per cent por ciento [por th-yento]; (percentage) el porcentaje [el porthen-takheh]

performance (theatre, etc.) la función [la foonth-yon], la representación [la repress-en-tath-yon] ➤ 83

perhaps quizá(s) [keetha(ss)], tal vez [tal beth]

permission permiso [permeeso]

person persona [perssona], el hombre [el ombreh]

Peruvian (man/woman) peruano/peruana [per-wano/per-wana]

petrol (Am: gas) gasolina [gassoleena], Arg: nafta [nafta] ➤ 23

petrol station (Am: gas station) gasolinera [gassoleenera], la estación de servicio [la esstath-yon deh serbeeth-yo] ➤ 23, 28

pharmacy farmacia [farmath-ya] ➤ 57, 60

phone n teléfono [telefono] ➤ 114; v telefonear [telefonay-ar], llamar por teléfono [yamar por telefono] ➤ 115

phone call llamada telefónica [yamada telefoneeka] ➤ 115

photo la foto(grafía) [la foto(grafee-a)]; (take a photo) hacer/sacar fotos [ather/sakar fotoss], fotografiar [fotografee-ar] ➤ 116

photographic equipment los artículos fotográficos [loss arteekooloss fotografeekoss] ➤ 56, 59

piece pieza [pyetha], trozo [trotho]

pillow almohada [almo-ada]

pity: it's a pity es una pena [ess oona pena]

place (location) el lugar [el loogar]

plain n (geog.) llanura [yanoora]

plant n planta [planta]

play v jugar [khoogar]

please por favor [por fabor] ➤12; (don't mention it) de nada [deh nada], no hay de qué [no ai deh keh]

pleased (pleased (with)) contento (de) [kontento (deh)], satisfecho (de) [sateessfecho (deh)], alegrarse (de) [alegrarsseh (deh)]; (to be pleased) estar contento [esstar kontento], estar satisfecho [esstar sateessfecho]

pleasure n el placer [el plather]

plus más [mass]

poison veneno [beneno]

poisoning el envenenamiento [el emben-ena-mee-ento], la intoxicación [la eentok-seekath-yon] ➤ 111

police policía [poleethee-a] ➤ 117

polite cortés [kortess]

politics política [poleeteeka]

poor (not rich) pobre [pobreh]

port (harbour) puerto [pwerto] ➤ 33, 81

position la posición [la posseeth-yon]

possible posible [posseebleh]

post office oficina de correos [ofeetheena deh kor-ayoss] ➤ 114

post v (mail) enviar [emb-yar] ➤ 114

postpone retardar [retardar]

pot (for cooking) olla [oya], cazuela [kathwela], puchero [poochero]

pottery alfarería [alfarer-ee-a], cerámica [theramee-ka]

prayer la oración [la orath-yon]

prefer preferir [prefereer]

pregnant embarazada [embarathada]

prescribe recetar [rethetar], prescribir [presskreebeer] ➤ 111

present (gift) regalo [regalo]; (to be present) estar presente [esstar pressenteh]

pretty adj guapo [gwapo], bonito [boneeto], lindo [leendo]

price precio [preth-yo]

priest el sacerdote [el satherdoteh], el cura [el koora]

prison la cárcel [la karthel] ➤ 118

prize premio [prem-yo]

DICTIONARY

probable   probable [probableh]

probably   probablemente [probable-menteh]

profession   la profesión [la professyon]

programme n (Am: program)   el programa [el programa]

promise n   promesa [promessa]

pronounce   pronunciar [pronoonth-yar]

protection   la protección [la protek-thyon]

public   público [poobleeko]

public holiday   el día de fiesta [el dee-a deh fyessta] **>** 18

public transport   el transporte público [el transporteh poobleeko] **>** 34

Puerto Rican (man/woman)   puertorriqueño/ puertorriqueña [pwerto-reekenyo/pwerto-reekenya]

pull v   tirar [teerar]

punishment   castigo [kassteego]

purse   cartera [kartera], Am: billetera [bee-yetera]

push v   empujar [empookhar], dar un golpe a [dar oon golpeh a]

put   poner [poner], colocar [kolokar]

Q

quality n   la calidad [la kaleedad]

question n   pregunta [pregoonta]; (problem) la cuestión [la kwesst-yon], el problema [el problema]

queue n   cola [kola]

quick adj, **quickly** adv   adj rápido [rapeedo], Am: ligero [leekhero]; adv rápidamente [rapeedamenteh], deprisa [depreessa]

quiet adj, **quietly** adv   adj tranquilo [trankeelo], quieto [kyeto]; adv bajo [bakho]; (talk quietly) en voz f baja [en both bakha]

quite   bastante [basstanteh]

R

radio   la radio [la rad-yo]

railway (railway/railroad) el ferrocarril [el ferokareel]; (line) línea [leenya]

rain v   llover [yober]

ramp   rampa [rampa]

rape n   la violación [la bee-olath-yon] **>** 117, 118

rare   raro [raro]

rarely   rara vez [rara beth], raramente [raramenteh]

rather   más bien [mass byen]

reach v   conseguir [konssegeer], lograr [lograr], alcanzar [alkanthar]

read v   leer [lay-er]

ready   listo [leessto]

realize   darse cuenta de [darsseh kwenta deh]

reason   la razón [la rathon], causa [kowssa]

receipt   recibo [retheebo]

receipt: make a receipt   dar recibo [dar retheebo]

receive   recibir [retheebeer]

recent adj   reciente [reth-yenteh]

recently adv   hace poco [atheh poko], Am: recién [ress-yen]; (the other day) el otro día [el otro dee-a]

reception   la recepción [la retheph-yon] **>** 69

recognize   reconocer [rekonother]

recommend   recomendar [rekomendar]

recover (after illness, etc.)   reponerse [reponersseh], descansar [desskanssar]

red   rojo [rokho]

reduction   rebaja [rebakha], descuento [desskwento] **>** 32

refuse v   rechazar [rechathar], rehusar [rayoossar]

region   la región [la rekh-yon], zona [thona]

register (baggage)   facturar [faktoorar]

registration   la recepción [la retheph-yon]

related (family)   pariente [paree-enteh], emparentado [emparentado]

reluctantly   de mala gana [deh mala gana]

remedy   remedio [remed-yo] **>** 60

remember   acordarse de [akordarsseh deh], recordar [rekordar]

remind s.o. of sth   recordar algo a alguien [rekordar algo a alg-yen]

rent n   el alquiler [el alkeeler] **>** 6, 29, 74

rental car   coche de alquiler [kocheh deh alkeeler] **>** 29

repair   v reparar [reparar]; n arreglo [areglo], la reparación [la reparath-yon] **>** 24

repeat v   repetir [repeteer]

replace   sustituir [sooss-teet-weer], reemplazar [reh-emplathar], reponer [reponer]; (replacement) repuesto [repwessto]

reply v   responder [ressponder], contestar [kontesstar]

request n   el favor [el fabor], ruego [rwego] **>** 12

reservation   reserva [resserba] **>** 6, 30, 69

residence (place of)   domicilio [domeetheel-yo], residencia [resseedenth-ya] **>** 22

responsible   responsable [ressponssableh]; (competent) competente [kompetenteh]

rest n   (break) descanso [desskansso]; (the rest) el resto [el ressto], las sobras [lass sobrass], los restos [loss resstoss]

restaurant   el restaurante [el resstow-ranteh] **>** 36

restless   intranquilo [eentrankeelo], inquieto [eenk-yeto]

result   resultado [ressooltado]

return   n vuelta [bwelta]; v volver [bolber]

ribbon   cinta [theenta]

rich (money)   rico [reeko]

right   (exact) exacto [ekssakto], preciso [pretheesso]; (correct) correcto [korekto]; (suitable, appropriate) adecuado [adekwado]; (to be right) tener razón f [tener rathon]; (on the right) a la derecha [a la derecha]

ring (doorbell, etc.)   tocar el timbre [tokar el teembreh]

risk n   riesgo [ree-ezgo]

river   río [ree-o]; (riverbank) orilla [oree-ya]

road map   el mapa de carreteras [el mapa deh kareterass] **>** 28

road sign   el indicador de camino [el eendeekador deh kameeno]

rock   roca [roka], peña [penya]

room   sala [sala]

rotten   podrido [podreedo]

round adj   redondo [redondo]

route   itinerario [eeteenerar-yo]

rubbish (Am: garbage) basura [bassoora]
rule n regla [regla]
run v (on foot) correr [korer]

S

sad triste [treessteh]; (sadness) pena [pena]
safety pin aguja de seguridad [agookha deh segooreedad]
sale n venta [benta]
Salvadorian (man/woman) salvadoreño/salvadoreña [salbadorenyo/salbadorenya]
same igual [eegwal]; (the same thing) lo mismo [lo meezmo]
satisfied satisfecho [sateessfecho], contento [kontento]
save v (a life, etc.) salvar [salbar]
say v decir [detheer]
scorpion el escorpión [el esskorp-yon]
Scotland Escocia [esskoth-ya]
Scots (man/woman) el escocés/la escocesa [el essko-thess/la essko-thessa]
sea el mar [el mar]
sea urchin erizo de mar [ereetho deh mar]
season (time of year) la estación [la esstath-yon] > 18; (football, etc) temporada [temporada]; (high season) temporada principal [temporada preentheepal]
seat asiento [assyento]
second n (time) segundo [segoondo]
secret adj secreto [sekreto]; (in secret) en secreto [en sekreto]
secretly secretamente [sekretamenteh]
security la seguridad [la segooreedad]
see v ver [ber]; (see again) volver a ver [bolber a ber]
self-service shop/store autoservicio [owto-serbeeth-yo]
send v enviar [emb-yar], mandar [mandar]
sender (package, etc.) el/la remitente [el/la remeetenteh] > 114
sentence (phrase) la frase [la frasseh]
separate adj separado [separado]
serious serio [ser-yo], grave [grabeh]
serve servir [serbeer]
service (relig.) servicio [serveeth-yo], oficio [ofeeth-yo] > 80; (mass) misa [meessa] > 80; (restaurant) servicio [serbeeth-yo]
service/rest station (motorway/highway) el albergue de carretera [el albergeh deh karetera]
settle (a matter) arreglar [areglar], terminar [termeenar]
severe (illness, etc.) grave [grabeh]
sex sexo [seksso]
shade (colour) tono [tono]
shades (sunglasses) las gafas de sol [lass gafass deh sol]
shameless (impertinent) descarado [desskarado], sinvergüenza [seem-berg-wentha]
she ella [aya]
ship barco [barko] > 33
shoe zapato [thapato] > 66

shop n tienda [tyenda]; (business) negocio [negoth-yo]; (to go shopping) ir de compras [eer deh komprass] > 54
shore orilla [oree-ya]
short corto [korto]; (person) bajo [bakho]; (shortage) falta [falta]
shot n (gun, etc.) tiro [teero]
shout v gritar [greetar]
show v enseñar [enssenyar], mostrar [mosstrar]; (indicate) indicar [eendeekar], señalar [senyalar]
shut v cerrar [therar]
shy tímido [teemeedo]
sick (Br: ill) enfermo [emfermo] > 110
side lado [lado]
sights (tourism) los monumentos [loss monoomentoss] > 79
sightseeing tour of a town/city visita de la ciudad [beesseeta deh la th-yoodad], la excursión [la ekss-koor-syon] > 78
sign n letrero [letrero]; (traffic) la señal [la senyal]
signature firma [feerma] > 106
silence n silencio [seelenth-yo], calma [kalma]; (silently) silenciosamente [seelenth-yo-samenteh], en silencio [en seelenth-yo]; (to be silent) callar [ka-yar]
since (time) desde [dezdeh]; (because) como [komo], ya que [ya keh], porque [porkeh]; (since when) ¿desde cuándo? [dezdeh kwando]
sing cantar [kantar]
single (relationship status) soltero [soltero] > 22
sister hermana [ermana]; (sister-in-law) cuñada [koonyada]
sit v (sit down) sentarse [sentarsseh]; (to be seated) estar sentado [esstar sentado]
situated: to be situated estar [esstar], encontrarse [enkontrarsseh], estar echado/acostado [esstar echado/akosstado]
situation la situación [la seet-wath-yon]
size tamaño [tamanyo]; (length) la longitud [la lonkheetood]; (height) altura [altoora]; (clothes) talla [ta-ya]; (hats, shirts, shoes) número [noomero]
sky cielo [th-yelo]
sleep v dormir [dormeer]
slim (thin) delgado [delgado], esbelto [ezbelto]
slow adj lento [lento]
slowly despacio [desspath-yo], lentamente [lentamenteh]
small pequeño [pekenyo]
small talk charla informal [charla eemformal] > 14
smell n el olor [el olor]; v oler [oler]
smoke fumar [foomar]
(non-)smoker (no) fumador/a m/f [(no) foomador/a]
smuggle v pasar de contrabando [passar deh kontrabando]
snack bar cafetería [kafeteree-a], el bar [el bar]; (on the beach) chiringuito [cheereengeeto]
snack n bocado [bokado], merienda [mer-yenda]
snow v nevar [nebar]
society la sociedad [la soth-yedad]

soft blando [blando]; (sound, colour) suave [swabeh]
solid (firm) firme [feermeh], fijo [feekho]
some algunos [algoonoss], unos [oonoss];
(somebody) alguien [alg-yen]; (something) algo [algo];
(sometimes) a veces [a bethess]
son hijo [eekho]
song la canción [la kanth-yon]
soon pronto [pronto]
sort n (kind) la clase [la klasseh]
sort out regular [regoolar], arreglar [areglar]
source (information, etc.) la fuente [la fwenteh]
south el sur [el soor]
South America Sudamérica [soodamereeka]
South American (man/woman) sudamericano/
sudamericana [soodamereekano/soodamereekana]
souvenir recuerdo [rekwerdo] ➤ 66
space el área [el araya]
Spain España [esspanya]
Spanish (~man/~woman) el español/la española
[el esspanyol/la esspanyola]; (language) español
[esspanyol]
speak hablar [ablar]
speed n la velocidad [la belotheedad]
spell v deletrear [dele-tray-ar]
spoiled (ruined) estropeado [esstropay-ado]
spoon cuchara [koochara]
sport el deporte [el deporteh] ➤ 85
sports field campo de deportes [kampo deh deportess]
spring, source (water) la fuente [la fwenteh]
square (town/city, etc.) plaza [platha]
staff el personal [el perssonal]
stairs, staircase escalera [esskalera]
stamp v (e.g. a ticket) franquear [frankay-ar] ➤ 114
stand v estar [esstar], estar de pie [esstar deh pyeh]
star estrella [esstraya]
start v comenzar [komenthar]
state (condition) estado [esstado];
(state) estado [esstado]
station la estación [la esstath-yon] ➤ 31
stationery n los artículos de escritorio [loss
arteekooloss deh esskreetor-yo] ➤ 67
stay v quedarse [kedarsseh]; n estancia [esstanth-ya],
Am: estadía [esstadee-a]
steal v robar [robar]
steep escarpado [esskarpado]
still (e.g. still more) todavía [todabee-a], aún [a-oon]
sting v pinchar [peenchar], picar [peekar]
stone piedra [pyedra]
stop v parar(se) [parar[seh]], detener(se)
[detener[seh]]; (bus stop, etc.) parada [parada] ➤ 35;
(stop!) ¡alto! [alto]
stopover/layover parada [parada]
store (Br: shop) tienda [tyenda];
(business) negocio [negoth-yo]
storm n tormenta [tormenta]
story (tale) cuento [kwento]
stove n estufa [esstoofa]
straight on todo seguido/derecho
[todo segeedo/derecho]

stranger forastero/forastera [forasstero/forasstera]
street (road) la calle [la ka-yeh]; (in the countryside)
carretera [karetera]
study v estudiar [esstood-yar]
stupid tonto [tonto], estúpido [esstoopeedo],
bobo [bobo], Am: zonzo [son-so]
style estilo [essteelo]
suburb las afueras [lass afwerass]
subway paso subterráneo [passo soobteranayo]
success éxito [ekseeto]
sudden adj, **suddenly** adv de repente [deh repenteh]
suitcase maleta [maleta]
sum (math.) suma [sooma]
summit la cumbre [la koombreh], cima [theema]
sun n, **sunny** adj n el sol [el sol]; adj soleado f [soledad]
sunglasses (shades) las gafas de sol [lass gafass deh sol]
supermarket supermercado [soopermerkado] ➤ 57
supplement n suplemento [sooplemento] ➤ 33
sure adj seguro [segooro], cierto [th-yerto]
surely ciertamente [th-yertamenteh]
surname el apellido [el apayeedo] ➤ 22
surprised sorprendido [sorprendeedo]
swear v insultar [eenssooltar]
sweat v sudar [soodar]
swim v la natación [la natath-yon] ➤ 84
swimming pool piscina [peess-theena],
Am: pileta [peeleta]
switch (light, etc.) el interruptor [el eenterooptor]
sympathy (condolences) el pésame [el pessameh]

T

table mesa [messa]
take part (in) tomar parte (en) [tomar parteh (en)]
take place tener lugar [tener loogar]
take v llevar(se) [yebar[seh]]; (bring along) llevar
consigo [yebar konsseego]; (take hold of) tomar
[tomar]; (the bus, etc.) ir en [eer en]
take-off el despegue [el desspegeh]
talk v hablar [ablar]
tall alto [alto]
taste n gusto [goossto], el sabor [el sabor];
v probar [probar]
tax impuesto [eempwessto], tributo [treebooto]
taxi el taxi [el taksee]
telephone n teléfono [telefono] ➤ 116; (telephone
line) la comunicación [la komooneekath-yon]
tell v contar [kontar]
temperature temperatura [temperatoora] ➤ 19
terrible horrible [oreebleh], terrible [tereebleh],
espantoso [esspantosso]
than (comparison) que [keh]
thank (s.o.) dar las gracias (a alg) [dar lass grath-yass
(a alg)], agradecer (a alg) [agradether (a alg-yen)]
➤ 12
thanks gracias [grath-yass]; (gratitude)
agradecimiento [agra-dethee-mee-ento] ➤ 12
that's why por esto/eso/ello [por essto/esso/ayo]
theatre teatro [tay-atro] ➤ 82
theft robo [robo] ➤ 118

their sing su [soo], pl sus [sooss]

then entonces [entonthess], después [desspwess];
(in that case) en ese caso [en esseh kasso]

there allí [a-yee], allá [a-ya];
(over there) ahí [a-ee]; (there is/are) hay [ai]

therefore por eso/esto/ello [por esso/essto/ayo]

they ellos [ayoss], ellas [ayass]

thin delgado [delgado]

thing cosa [kossa]

think pensar [penssar]

thirsty: to be thirsty tener sed [tener sed]

this/these, that/those
  close to speaker: (this) este m [essteh], esta f [essta];
  (these) estos m [esstoss], estas f [esstass];
  not close to speaker: (that) ese m [esseh], esa f [essa];
  (those) esos m [essoss], esas f [essass]; **further away**
  from speaker: (that) aquel m [akel], aquella f [akaya];
  (those) aquellos [akayoss], aquellas [akayass]

thought n pensamiento [penssa-mee-ento],
  idea [eedaya]

through (prep) por [por], a través de [a trabess deh];
  (by means of) mediante [med-yanteh]

ticket el billete [el bee-yeteh], Am: boleto [boleto]
  ➤ 33, 35; entrada [entrada] ➤ 83

ticket office taquilla [takee-ya],
  Am: boletería [boleteree-a] ➤ 83

time n tiempo [tyempo] ➤ 16;
  (time of day) hora [ora] ➤ 16;
  (instance: one time) la vez [la beth];
  (two times) dos veces [doss bethess]

time: in/on time (in time) a tiempo [a tyempo],
  oportunamente [oportoonamenteh];
  (on time) puntual [poont-wal];
  adv puntualmente [poont-walmenteh]

timetable horario [orar-yo] ➤ 31, 33

tip (Am: gratuity) propina [propeena] ➤ 35, 40

tired cansado [kanssado]

tiring fatigoso [fateegosso]

to a [a], en [en]; (to London) a Londres [a londress]

tobacco tabaco [tabako]

today hoy [oy]

together adv en común [en komoon], juntos
  [khoontoss], juntas [khoontass]

toilet el baño [el banyo], el servicio
  [el serbeeth-yo] ➤ 37, 70, 72, 118

toilet paper el papel higiénico [el papel eekh-yeneeko]

tolerate (put up with) soportar [soportar]

tomorrow mañana [manyana]

tone (sound) sonido [soneedo]

too much/many demasiado [demass-yado]

topic (of a conversation, etc.) asunto [assoonto],
  el tema [el tema]

tour n visita [beesseeta] ➤ 78

tour guide guía m/f [gee-a]

tourist information office oficina de turismo
  [ofeetheena deh tooreezmo]

tow (away) remolcar [remolkar] ➤ 24

towards (direction) hacia [ath-ya]

town la ciudad [la th-yoodad]

town centre centro (de la ciudad) [thentro
  (deh la th-yoodad)]

town hall ayuntamiento [a-yoonta-mee-ento] ➤ 81

toy n el juguete [el khoo-geteh]

traffic tráfico [trafeeko]

train n el tren [el tren] ➤ 31

transfer v (money) transferir [transsfereer]

transit visa visado de tránsito [beessado deh
  transseeto]

translate traducir [tradootheer]

travel agency agencia de viajes
  [akhenth-ya deh bee-akhess]

travel v viajar [bee-akhar]

traveller's cheque/check el cheque de viaje
  [el chekeh deh bee-akheh] ➤ 106

tree el árbol [el arbol]

trip n la excursión [la ekss-koor-syon] ➤ 81

truck el camión [el kam-yon]

true verdad [berdad]

try v intentar [eententar], probar [probar]

tunnel el túnel [el toonel]

typical (of) típico (de) [teepeeko (deh)]

U

ugly feo [fayo]

umbrella el paraguas [el para-gwass]

uncertain incierto [eenth-yerto]

uncle tío [tee-o]

unconscious desmayado [dezma-yado],
  desvanecido [dessba-netheedo], sin conocimiento
  [seen konothee-mee-ento] ➤ 112

under bajo [bakho], debajo de [debakho deh]

underground (railway) metro [metro], Am:
  subterráneo [soobterranayo] ➤ 34

understand entender [entender]

underway (in transit) en (el) camino [en (el)
  kameeno], en el viaje [en el bee-akheh], de viaje
  [deh bee-akheh]

uneasy inquieto [eenk-yeto],
  incómodo [eenkomodo]

unfortunately desgraciadamente
  [dez-grath-yada-menteh]

unfriendly antipático [anteepateeko]

unhappy infeliz [eem-feleeth]

unhealthy malsano [malssano]

United States Estados Unidos [esstadoss ooneedoss]

unknown forastero [forasstero],
  desconocido [desskonotheedo]

unlucky desgraciado [dez-grath-yado]

until hasta [assta]

up prep arriba [areeba]

urgent urgente [oor-khen-teh];
  (hurried) de prisa [deh preessa]

Uruguayan (man/woman) uruguayo/uruguaya
  [ooroogwa-yo/ooroogwa-ya]

us nos [noss];
  (to us) a nosotros [a nossotross]

use v usar [oossar], emplear [emplay-ar]

V

vacant (bathroom, etc.) libre [leebreh]

vacation las vacaciones [lass bakath-yoness]

vain: in vain en balde [en baldeh]

valid válido [baleedo] ➤ 22

value n el valor [el balor]

vegetables las verduras [lass berdoorass] ➤ 41, 50, 64; (pulses) las legumbres [lass legoombress]

Venezuelan (man/woman) venezolano/venezolana [benetholano/benetholana]

versus contra [kontra]

very muy [mwee]; (very much/many) mucho [moocha]

view n vista [beessta] ➤ 70

village aldea [aldaya], pueblo [pweblo]

visa visado [beessado], Am: visa [beessa] ➤ 22

visible visible [beesseebleh]

visit v visitar [beesseetar]; (visit s.o.) visitar a alg [beesseetar a alg-yen], ir a ver a alg [eer a ber a alg-yen]

voice la voz [la both]

volume (book) tomo [tomo]

vote v elegir [elekheer]

W

wage (salary) sueldo [sweldo], salario [salar-yo], paga [paga]

wait for esperar [essperar]

waiter/waitress camarero/camarera [kamarero/kamarera], Am: mozo/moza [mosso/mossa]

waiting room sala de espera [sala deh esspera] ➤ 113

wake v despertar [desspertar]

Wales Gales [galess]

walk v ir a pie [eer a pyeh], andar [andar]; (to go for a walk) pasear [passay-ar]

wallet cartera [kartera] ➤ 117

want v querer [kerer], desear [dessay-ar]

war guerra [gera]

warm adj caliente [kal-yenteh]

warn v (warn about/of) advertir de [ad-berteer deh]; (warn against) prevenir (contra) [prebeneer (kontra)]

warning! ¡atención! [atenth-yon], ¡cuidado! [kweedado]

wash v lavar [labar]

watch n el reloj de pulsera [el relokh deh poolssera]; v estar mirando [esstar meerando]

water (el) agua [(el) agwa]; (drinking water) (el) agua potable [(el) agwa potableh]

way (of doing something) modo [modo], manera [manera]; (route) camino [kameeno], ruta [roota]

we nosotros [nossotross]

weak débil [debeel]

wear v llevar (puesto) [yebar (pwessto)]

weather tiempo [tyempo] ➤ 19

web address la dirección de internet [la deerek-thyon deh eenternet] ➤ 8

wedding boda [boda]

week semana [semana] ➤ 17

weigh v pesar [pessar]

weight peso [pesso]

welcome! ¡bienvenido! [byem-ben-eedo]

well adv bien [byen]; (interjection) bueno [bweno], pues [pwess]

Welsh (man/woman) el galés/la galesa [el galess/la galessa]

west el oeste [el o-essteh]

wet mojado [mokhado]; (soaking wet) empapado [empapado]; (damp, humid) húmedo [oomedo]

what? ¿qué? [keh]; (what for?) ¿para qué? [para keh]

wheelchair silla de ruedas [see-ya deh rwedass]

when cuando [kwando]

where dónde [dondeh]; (where from) ¿de dónde? [deh dondeh]; (where to) ¿a dónde? [adondeh]

whether si [see]

which ¿cuál? [kwal]

while mientras (que) [mee-entrass (keh)]

white blanco [blanko]

who?, to whom? ¿quién? [kyen]; ¿a quién? [a kyen]

whose? ¿de quién? [deh kyen]

why? ¿por qué? [por keh]

wide ancho [ancho]

wife esposa [esspossa], la mujer [la mookher]

win v ganar [ganar]

wish v desear [dessay-ar]

with con [kon]

within (time) en [en], dentro de [dentro deh]

without sin [seen]

witness n testigo [tessteego]

woman señora [senyora]

wood (timber) madera [madera]

word palabra [palabra]

work v trabajar [trabakhar]; (function) funcionar [foonth-yonar]

working days los días laborables [loss dee-ass laborabless]

workshop el taller [el ta-yer] ➤ 24, 27

world mundo [moondo]

worry n la preocupación [la prayokoo-path-yon]; (to worry about) preocuparse por/de [prayo-koo-parsseh por/deh]

worth: to be worth a lot valer mucho [baler moocho]

write escribir [esskreebeer]; (in writing) por escrito [por esskreeto]

wrong adj falso [falsso], incorrecto [eenkorekto]; (to be wrong) equivocarse [ekeebo-karsseh]

Y

year año [anyo]

yellow amarillo [amaree-yo]

you (formal) sing usted [oossted]; (to you); a usted [a oossted]; pl ustedes [oosstedess]; (to you) a ustedes [a oosstedess]

you (informal) sing tú [too]; (to you) a ti [a tee]; pl vosotros/as [bossotross/ass]; (to you) a vosotros/as [a bossotross/ass]

young joven [khoben]

your sing/inf tu [too]; sing/formal su [soo]; pl/inf vuestro/a [bwesstro/a]; pl/formal su [soo]

youth hostel el albergue juvenil [el albergeh khoo-ben-eel]

A Little Confession...

Translating English expressions directly into foreign languages is often dangerous – and Spanish is no exception. If you're in a shop and want to ask how much something costs, don't translate the phrase "how much?" too literally. Although *cómo* [komo] does mean "how" and *mucho* [moocho] really is the word for "much", if you go up to the shopkeeper and proudly say *como mucho* [komo mucho], all you'll get is a funny look – you'll have just confided in them that you eat a lot! Try *¿cuánto costa?* [kwanto kossta] instead.

Embarrassed?

If you make the mistake above, don't compound the situation by committing this next linguistic crime. If you've slipped up with your Spanish and the blood is rushing to your cheeks, don't grab desperately for the nearest English-sounding word: saying you're *embarazada* [embarathada] will make things worse: it actually means you're pregnant. The correct way to say "I'm embarrassed" is *tengo vergüenza* [tengo vergoo-entha] (lit: I have shame).

A! O! Let's go!

A great deal of Spanish words end with the letters "o" and "a". This can be a great help, as words ending in "o" are usually masculine, and words ending in "a" are very often feminine. With so many words ending in these two vowels, however, it's quite possible to get mixed up – and if you do, you might just find yourself in some very sticky linguistic situations. If you're trying to order chicken in a restaurant, for instance, and say *polla* [poya] instead of *pollo* [poyo] to your waiter, you'll actually be asking for a plateful of a particularly male part of the anatomy. The same goes for the Spanish word for fox: *zorro* [zoro]. If you spot one in the woods and loudly point it out to a passer-by, make sure you don't say *zorra* [zora] instead – it's the Spanish word for "bitch".

It's Rude to Point...

If you're in a bar and want to look cool by ordering another drink with a casual wave of your hand, be careful how you proceed. Whatever you do, don't stretch out your index finger, clench the rest of your hand into a fist, and show the bartender the back of your hand. If you do this, you're more likely to get thrown out of the establishment than be served another drink: it's the Spanish equivalent of showing someone your middle finger.

An Innocent Question?

The wavy symbol that appears over the letter 'n' in some Spanish words (ñ) might look small and insignificant – but ignore it at your peril. If you want to ask someone how old they are, for instance, the Spanish sentence you'll need is: *¿Cuántos años tienes?* [kwantoss anyoss tyeness]. If you fail to pronounce the ñ and say *anos* [anoss] instead of años [anyoss], however, it'll be a completely different question altogether: "How many anuses do you have?" Don't say we didn't warn you!